MW00358881

THE WEST BRANCH MILL OF THE
SIERRA
LUMBER COMPANY

THE WEST BRANCH MILL OF THE
SIERRA
LUMBER COMPANY

EARLY LOGGING *in* NORTHEASTERN CALIFORNIA

Andy Mark

Charleston   London

THE
History
PRESS

Published by The History Press
Charleston, SC 29403
www.historypress.net

First published 2012

ISBN 978.1.5402.2123.0

Library of Congress CIP data applied for.

CONTENTS

ACKNOWLEDGEMENTS

Most of all, I would like to thank my wife, Jill, for her support, patience and perceptive observations throughout the project. Her constant encouragement was crucial.

Special thanks to Dale Wangberg, his brother Rob and his mother, Ida, who were very generous with their photographic collection. Dale offered assistance in other ways, as well. Perry Sims also went out of his way to contribute a very important photo connected to my research.

George Thompson and his staff at California State University, Chico (CSUC), Special Collections, were a tremendous help. Deborah Besnard, in particular, directed me to some important photos, while other staff members accommodated my many requests to access rare resources. I would also like to thank Michael Watts and the staff in CSUC's microfilm room for their assistance. Scott Sherman, reference librarian at Tehama County Library, Red Bluff, was extremely gracious and helpful with his time. Kathleen Correia, supervising librarian of the history section of the California State Library, Sacramento, was very generous with photographic permission. Susan Snyder, head of public services at Bancroft Library, UC Berkeley, helped guide me through the process of obtaining some valuable photos from the Bancroft collection. The staff at the Gold Nugget Museum, in Paradise, helped with research and offered interesting information.

Lucy Sperlin and Nancy Brower, of the Butte County Historical Society, offered suggestions and located a photograph for me. Brett Nichols, from the Superior Court in Oroville, provided access to some very informative court records. Anna Ciesla, from Butte County Pubic Works, sent me reproductions of some very useful official Butte County maps.

Robyn Scibilio, site manager at Genetic Resource and Conservation Center (GRCC), Chico, gave me her time and some handouts describing the history of the GRCC. Michael Suplita, from the Center for Economic Development, CSUC, provided information about Enloe Medical Center employment numbers. Terry Collins gave me his time and furnished printed material about Collins Almanor Forest.

John Rudderow pointed me in the direction of some excellent flume references. Richard Burrill offered suggestions and provided some good background information, in general. My niece, Sue Fortner, clarified some questions I had about horses.

I would like to thank Aubrie Koenig, commissioning editor for The History Press, for her recommendations on how to improve the manuscript and assistance in submitting it. I also appreciate the effort that Darcy Mahan, project editor for The History Press, went through in helping me make it more presentable.

Glenn Dietz, Fred Young, Alzora Snyder and Ruth Hughes Hitchcock generously donated historical photos to California State University, Chico, Special Collections. Glenn Dietz donated photos to the Tehama County Library, at Red Bluff, as well.

The late John Nopel, a well-known and highly regarded Butte County historian, conducted extensive research on the flume and also donated photos to the university. His work was very much appreciated and made mine a lot easier.

Last, but not least, I would like to extend special appreciation to the preeminent logging historian, the late W.H. Hutchinson. As I combed through the many resources for my research, "Hutch's" name was referenced far more than anyone else. He was clearly the ultimate authority on old-time logging in northeastern California.

My apologies to anyone who provided assistance that I may have failed to acknowledge.

INTRODUCTION

Hidden below the steep, rocky walls of Big Chico Creek Canyon, located in the foothills east of Chico, California, lies a story of hardy men who, at the turn of the twentieth century, often risked life and limb to help shape the growing western frontier. Today, this country is mostly inaccessible by vehicle, except to Sierra Pacific Industries and the loggers who still carry on the tradition of harvesting trees to supply a perpetually hungry lumber economy.

Much has been written about logging in California, in general, but the West Branch Mill operations in this canyon have received relatively little attention, except for photographs that have been handed down to descendants of those bygone times, who have, in turn, made them available to the public. The lack of detailed information about the mill is somewhat surprising, however, considering that at one time, it was reported that the lumber company paid out more money for labor than any other industry in Butte County, primarily because of the West Branch Mill.

I spend quite a bit of my leisure time mountain biking and hiking in the canyon. Since I have an interest in local history, it was just a matter of time before I wanted to know more about this large mill built along the creek that operated over one hundred years ago. Fortunately, Butte County historians W.H. Hutchinson and John Nopel gave me a starting point, and I took it from there. I felt the only way to get unique stories about this place was to literally go back in time by reading what the newspapers then had to say about it. These news clippings that I collected from countless hours of scanning through microfilm make up the bulk of my resource materials.

This book focuses on the West Branch Mill but begins with logging in northeastern California in general in the years prior to the canyon lumber operations. It ends with the national concern over forest devastation that resulted from uninhibited logging practices that actually began in the eastern states but rapidly spread westward.

The stories in between are not just about the mill, although they are always related to it in some way or another. For instance, the valley town of Chico is well represented. The rough-cut lumber from the mill was sent down a twenty-five-mile-long flume to the Chico factory, which specialized in fruit box and tray stock and more. Injured loggers were sometimes sent in makeshift boats down this same waterway in order to receive the best medical attention in the valley. There was essentially only one way to get to the mill from the valley, and that was on the Humboldt Wagon Road, whose hard, bumpy surface, especially at the beginning of the foothills, made for an exhausting trip on the stage.

There are plenty of engaging people in the book. Perhaps the most well known MD in northern California history, Dr. Newton T. Enloe, began his California practice as the resident physician for this mill. I hope to show that some lesser-known individuals, such as mill superintendents Barney Cussick and Frank Thatcher, were also heroes in their own right. John Bidwell, Chico's founder and principal landowner, plays a significant role in this book too.

Sit back and relax. Read how the West was won from a vegetative viewpoint. The "jackies" were a lively bunch, and you'll have a whole new perspective on what it was like to live in the foothills of northeastern California at the turn of the twentieth century.

CHAPTER 1
BEFORE THE WEST BRANCH MILL

B efore the gold rush, there was only a sprinkling of lumber mills scattered about what is now known as northeastern California. However, after massive numbers of settlers started pouring into the new territory looking to make fortunes mining for the bright yellow mineral, mountains rich in another resource provided the newcomers with an alternative way to become wealthy. The material was called "timber" and was often referred to as "green gold."

Many of the people who failed to make their fortunes in mining, along with others who never prospected, chose other occupations that became available—like ranching, farming, logging and selling mercantile, to name just a few. Mining camps, logging camps, homesteads and towns were springing up everywhere, and wherever people settled, the demand for lumber increased correspondingly. The timber for building was readily available for local consumption, and small lumber mills were quickly erected to service these nearby places. However, selling lumber to the larger city markets was simply out of reach because of transportation problems that competing coastal mills, which took advantage of conveniently located major waterways, such as the Pacific Ocean, did not have to contend with. In northeastern California, use of the Sacramento River to transport lumber met only limited success due to its meandering and unpredictable nature.

During the very early years, timber operations in the upper foothills and lower mountains east of Chico and Red Bluff,[1] located in the northeastern portion of the Sacramento Valley, were mostly dependent upon the forces of gravity and animal power to move the wood from place to place. After the hardworking fallers undermined a tree's natural ability to stay upright, gravity was responsible for getting it to the ground. The tree was then limbed and "bucked" into desirable lengths. Oxen or horse teams would then drag, referred to as "yard," the fallen timber to the next destination, generally a log "landing." If the terrain was suitable for it, logs were strung together and dragged by the animal teams to be placed in "log chutes," some of which allowed the downward forces of nature to once more make it easier to transport the fallen timber to a landing.

The chutes were simple in design. They were just long troughs, with sides made up of peeled tree trunks placed end to end, often supported at regular intervals by notched cross logs. Animals and, later, steam power were used to pull strings of logs along the chutes, which provided a smoother surface to slide the cut timber than soft or uneven ground, especially when the trough

Sketch of a gravity chute in Big Chico Creek Canyon. Drawn by Will L. Taylor, circa 1877. *Courtesy of CSU, Chico, Meriam Library, Special Collections. Donated by W.H. Hutchinson. Permission to reproduce granted by the California History Room, California State Library, Sacramento, California.*

was lubricated with grease or water at locations where the logs might have a tendency to get stuck. (The cable was attached to the rear of the log train, so the transported timber was actually being pushed.) However, in "gravity" chutes, also referred to as "running" chutes, logs rushed down precipitous slides at frighteningly high speeds, often crashing into others at the bottom of the incline. The steep topography of Big Chico Creek Canyon, located in California's northern part of Butte County and southern part of Tehama County, in the foothills northeast of Chico, was ideal for utilizing gravity chutes in the woods.

From the landing, the logs were often loaded onto "trucks" that rode on "tramways." A tramway was a light railway, consisting of either sawn timber or steel rails secured to cross planks or ties. These, in turn, were mounted on stringers that often rested on a cribbing designed to maintain a constant grade. To prevent wear, strap iron was frequently placed on the wooden rails. Again, bovines or equines provided the power to move the lumber along the tramways to a nearby mill. From the mills, animals hauled lumber wagons to market, typically in the valley, often over steep and rough roads.

Sketch of logs being roaded on tramway to Belmont Mill, near the headwaters of Big Chico Creek. Drawn by Will L. Taylor, circa 1877. *Courtesy of CSU, Chico, Meriam Library, Special Collections. Donated by W.H. Hutchinson. Permission to reproduce granted by the California History Room, California State Library, Sacramento, California.*

As reliable as they were, hauling with oxen or horses (or sometimes mules) was slow. Since time is money, transporting lumber this way was relatively expensive. Eventually, however, new technological advancements were made available to the lumbermen in the mountains of northeastern California that allowed the mills located within the vast stands of valuable sugar and ponderosa pine to compete with their coastal counterparts in the timber industry.

The first major boost for the lumber industry working in the foothills east of the upper Sacramento Valley was the California and Oregon Railroad, which came to Chico in the year 1870 and then continued its northbound journey up to Redding, arriving there in 1872. With this advancement, at least the mills located in the timber belt east of Chico and Red Bluff could get their products to the larger markets of Marysville, Sacramento and San Francisco once they arrived in the valley.

However, there was still that problem of getting the lumber down to the valley in a more economical way than with teams of slow, plodding beasts pulling wagons weighted down with stacks of lumber. Eventually, a man named C.F. Ellsworth, who was also known for constructing the first logging tramway in the northern Sierra, introduced the lumbermen east of Chico and Red Bluff to a technological innovation that revolutionized lumber transportation in this part of the country—the V-flume. This kind of waterway was first successfully used by a man called J.W. Haines to transport lumber from the eastern slope of the Sierra Nevada down to Carson City, Nevada, to be used in silver mines, after the silver strikes of 1859.

The V-flume was typically built to be about sixteen inches wide at the bottom, forty-eight inches across at water level and have thirty-two-inch sloping sides. This kind of transport system was an improvement over its square-box predecessor because not only did it require less lumber to build and less water to operate, but also in the event that floating planks would start to jam, water would back up so that the lumber would be lifted into the expanded upper section of the waterway and be freed to move on. That is, it was self-clearing, although not always.

Therefore, flume tender stations were located at various points along the flume. The stations were living quarters for the tenders and their families, if they had one. The flume tender's job was to repair the flume when necessary and to clear any jams that could not be freed naturally, often using a long-handled tool called a "pick-a-roon" that was designed to hook or stick into wood. The flume attendant was on constant watch to detect jams and had to be ready to respond immediately. For nighttime vigilance, a common practice was to hang a tin can from a rope to make sure the lumber was still moving along. If the can stopped rattling, it was the lumber herder's job to

Early Logging in Northeastern California

Lumber jam on V-flume, location unknown. *Courtesy of Tehama County Library, Red Bluff. Donated by Glenn Dietz, from Coyle Turner collection.*

Flume tender and possibly his wife at one of the stations in Big Chico Creek Canyon. *Courtesy of CSU, Chico, Meriam Library, Special Collections. Donated by Glenn Dietz.*

make his way along the narrow catwalks that ran alongside the waterway and fix the problem. Needless to say, this was an occupation fraught with perils, as the walkways were often wet or icy, and in many places, they were close to one hundred feet high.

Lumber wasn't the only material that was transported on the flume. Shakes and cordwood for fuel often made the trip too. Fish catches and venison would be sent from the mountains to friends below. Before telephones were installed in mountain locations, the flume would often be used as a message carrier, bringing down orders for supplies or requests for doctors. One of the most important roles of the flume was to act as a one-way highway for ambulance rafts, which carried injured people from the foothills or mountains to the valley below, where they could receive the best medical attention as quickly as possible.

Mr. Ellsworth owned the Empire Mill in Butte Meadows, east of Big Chico Creek, and, realizing that transportation to the valley was simply too expensive, experimented with ways to get lumber down to the valley more efficiently. When he proposed the possibility of building a V-flume down Big Chico and Butte Creeks, a local surveyor informed him that the steep, rocky canyon walls could not accommodate one. Ellsworth decided to sell his mill in Butte County and move up to Tehama County, possibly because he felt the terrain was more suitable for building one of these waterways. He eventually bought the Belle Mill, near Lyman Springs, and embarked on the bold venture from there. It took three years to build the forty-mile lumber highway, called the Empire flume, from his mill to the valley terminus at Sesma, and most of this time the locals would refer to it as "Ellsworth's Folly." The flume originally went to Sesma because it was the best place to meet with the California and Oregon Railroad, which, at Red Bluff, was on the west side of the Sacramento River. At the time, it was felt that the pontoon toll bridge there was too expensive and risky of a connection. As expensive as it was to build, the flume was completed in 1873 and eventually turned out to be a great success. Unfortunately, Ellsworth wasn't around to see his idea get the full respect it deserved. While supervising one of the final pieces of construction, he fell twenty feet from a trestle, eventually dying from his injuries.

The construction of the Empire flume inspired the construction of more flumes in California's northeastern foothills, including one north of it called the Blue Ridge flume, which originally started from Clipper Mill, located on the south fork of Digger Creek, and terminated where Ink's Creek meets the east side of the Sacramento River, north of Red Bluff, in 1874. To get its product to the other side of the river, the company's high-grade lumber was hauled by wagon on Jelly's Ferry, and the lower grade was floated down the

Early Logging in Northeastern California

river to Red Bluff to be captured by the "river-pigs" who pulled the wood out of the water, loaded it on wagons and sent it uphill to the planing mill on the west side of the river. Eventually, the Centennial Free Bridge was built to cross the river at Red Bluff in 1876, and the Blue Ridge flume, by then owned by Sierra Flume and Lumber Company, was soon extended to the banks opposite the town, where a new factory was built. Here the lumber was moved by rail over the bridge to the west side of the Sacramento River.

Colonel H.B. Shackelford, surveyor of Tehama County, felt that a flume could be built through Big Chico Creek Canyon, after all. So, in 1872, the Butte Flume and Lumber Company was formed to erect one and bring lumber down to the valley from the Cascade Mill, located in Chico Meadows (near Butte Meadows). During construction, the Belmont Mill and Arcade Mill (owned by J.N. McCormick) were built downstream to also take advantage of this new mode of lumber transportation. In the summer of 1874, the thirty-three-mile flume was completed to a point at the base of the foothills just outside of Chico, which was referred to as the "dump" or "Dumpville" because that was where the lumber was unloaded from the flume and stacked for drying. At the time, the flume did not get any closer to town, nearer to the railroad, because Butte Flume and Lumber chose not to pay the high cost of the right-of-way.[2]

At one time, the dump was a thriving community that included a hotel, a sash and door plant and a planing mill, along with some homes, shacks and bunkhouses. It also had a community outdoor platform for holding dances, which became a popular spot for people from Chico to come out and have a good time. In the summer of 1876, the flume was extended three and a half miles to a new dumping location along what is now East Eighth Street, in Chico. Despite the sudden loss of business, the sash and door factory at the old dump continued to run for a while, supplied with lumber from mills not connected to the flume.[3] It wasn't long before the residents of the community decided to refer to their town as Oakvale, because they felt the former designation sounded a bit offensive. The little town of Oakvale finally met the same fate as many other small lumber communities—it burned to the ground, and for many years afterward, there was little evidence of it left. Now even that scant evidence is buried under the developed area around the Canyon Oaks Country Club.

It was General John Bidwell, principal landowner and founder of Chico, who made the extension of the flume possible by purchasing the necessary land to move it beyond the old dumpsite. The new owners of the lumber company and flume, Sierra Flume and Lumber Company (who also swallowed up the Blue Ridge and N.L. Drew, formerly Empire, flume and lumber mill companies, with a few other individual mills, as well, including the

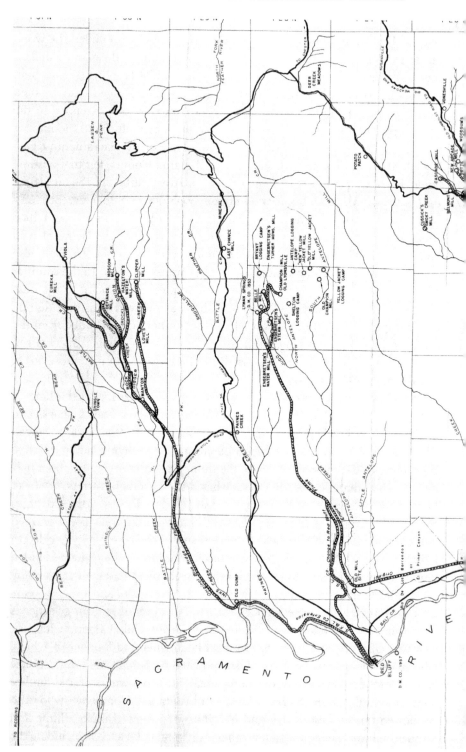

Early Logging in Northeastern California

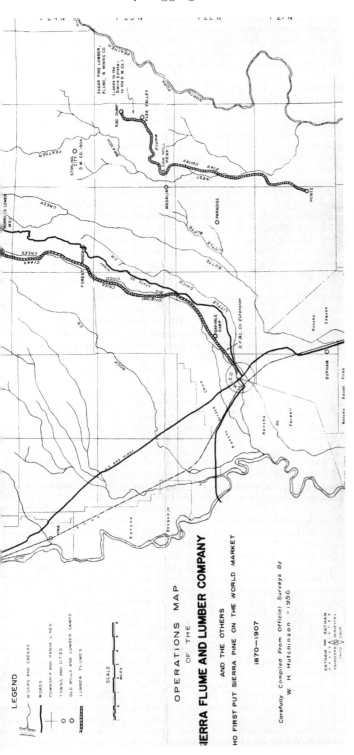

Map of lumber flumes in the foothills of northeastern Sacramento Valley, from 1870 to 1907, compiled by W.H. Hutchinson. *Courtesy of CSU, Chico, Meriam Library, Special Collections.*

Left: John Bidwell, from George C. Mansfield's 1918 book *History of Butte County California with Biographical Sketches of the Leading Men and Women of the County Who Have Been Identified with Its Growth and Development from the Early Days to the Present.*

Below: Official map of Butte County in 1877, showing the location of the old dump and where the flume entered the edge of Chico at the new site, East Eighth and Pine Streets. Note the California and Oregon Railroad tracks in southwest Chico. To the east of the flume can be seen the beginning of the Humboldt Wagon Road, which provided access to lumber in the foothills and mountains. *Courtesy of Butte County Public Works.*

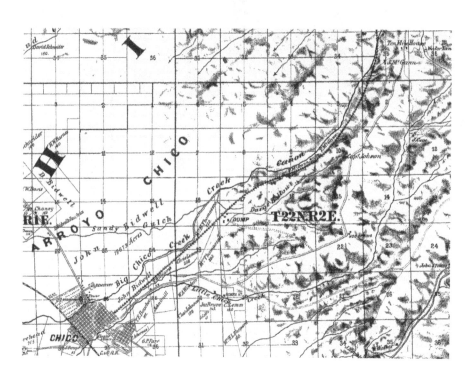

Early Logging in Northeastern California

The dumping station along what is now East Eighth Street, in Chico. Note how the flume turned sharply to head north along what is now Pine Street. *Courtesy of CSU, Chico, Meriam Library, Special Collections. Donated by Glenn Dietz.*

Arcade), certainly appreciated the important new right-of-way that Bidwell gave to them. It seems, however, that there was more to the land acquisition move than just locating the dumping station and lumber factory closer to the railroad and providing a stimulus to the economy of Chico.[4] The general had a plan. After the lumber was removed from the flume at the factory, the water had to go somewhere—it couldn't be released there, or it would flood that section of town. Therefore, the flume turned north from the factory, along what is now Pine Street, back toward Big Chico Creek. John Bidwell arranged to have the waterway connected to his own flume so that the lumber company's discharge water could help provide power to turn the waterwheel at the Chico Flour Mill, the general's enterprise located on the north side of the creek.[5] Even after the water was no longer used for the gristmill, it still provided water to irrigate various points on the north side of the creek.

When the factory at the new dump was finally built at the end of 1876, it wasn't long before a major controversy broke out. Although the people of Chico were originally under the impression that the new jobs created would be given to local white men and boys, it soon became apparent that quite a few Chinese workers were going to be hired, to the exclusion of white labor.

When forty-five Chinese men arrived from San Francisco, with the prospect of more on the way, Sierra Flume and Lumber—and a Mr. H.O. Hooper, who was leasing the factory at the time—was clearly falling into disfavor with the local people, who by then were feeling quite betrayed. There was talk of possible violence in the streets, but cooler heads prevailed...at first.[6] Instead, a formal letter of complaint addressed to General N.P. Chipman, general superintendent of the lumber company, appeared in a local paper. The writers of the petition appealed to the man in charge to change his position, pointing out that hiring white help was more prosperous to the community and asserting that the Chinese were undesirable "people who claim no affinity with us as American citizens."[7] Chipman's reply, printed in the same paper two weeks later, explained that, although he sympathized with the mass of concerned Chico citizens, the company's survival was at stake and that Chinese, with few exceptions, were only employed in positions in which white people were not skilled enough to perform or could not be depended upon to be permanent.[8] Chipman did not waver, so by the time the sash factory operations were well underway about a month later, there were thirty white men and forty-eight Chinese working at the plant.[9]

While the sash factory's policy of hiring Chinese over whites wasn't the only agitator of anti-Chinese sentiment in the community, it was certainly a major contributor. Anti-Chinese violence erupted soon afterward, targeting not only Chinese but also some of their employers, including John Bidwell. A wave of arsons and other terrorist behavior struck the town, including one incident in which the flume was vandalized and another in which a Chinese man near the flume was struck in the head with a rock by some boys. Finally, four innocent Chinese workers were brutally murdered (two others managed to survive) at a ranch near town. Chico became nationally recognized as a town whose lawlessness had gotten out of hand. The negative image threatened its chances of becoming a growing and prosperous community, as people feared the potential loss of insurance coverage and future investors. The town managed to survive the ordeal, but not without the citizens having to reconsider the consequences of their non-actions in allowing anti-Chinese thugs to roam free and do as they pleased.

When the plant burned down over a year later, in 1878, the lack of help in putting out the flames showed how Chico's townsfolk still resented the lumber company's continuing policy of hiring a high percentage of Chinese laborers. Many observers even said they were glad to see it burn.[10] It didn't help that this negative image was reinforced by the fact that Sierra Flume and Lumber was already being considered by many to be a huge monopoly that was driving smaller mills out of business.

Early Logging in Northeastern California

The use of the flume reduced the cost of transporting lumber to Chico from $12.00 per thousand board feet (M) by wagon to $1.50 M, which amounted to about a $5.00 M savings to the consumer. Its completion may have inspired the resurvey of the Butte-Tehama County boundaries in 1874, which placed the three sawmills and about nine miles of flume in Tehama County, an area that was formerly considered to be in Butte. It's been suggested that tax revenues may have prompted the border realignment.

V-flumes were truly engineering marvels of their time. They snaked through winding canyons. They crossed over steep gorges, with seemingly little surface area that was adequate for support. Sometimes the flume rested on cribbing close to the ground, other times the trestles rose as high as one hundred feet above the ground—whatever it took to try to maintain a somewhat constant grade. While these massive structures were well braced below with a strong wood framework, sometimes it was necessary to further support the more unstable sections with cables tied to trees, to reduce swaying.

It wasn't long after the Chico Creek flume was completed that the Butte Flume and Lumber Company began to consider liability issues. Therefore,

Sometimes the more unstable parts of the flume were further supported with cables, seen on the right-hand side of image. This photo was taken near the town of Oakvale. *Courtesy of CSU, Chico, Meriam Library, Special Collections. Donated by John Nopel.*

it felt compelled to post a notice in the September 18, 1874 edition of the *Northern Enterprise* newspaper: "TO ALL WHOM IT MAY CONCERN, Notice is hereby given, that the Butte Flume & Lumber Co. absolutely forbid all persons from riding down their flume. Offenders will be prosecuted to the full extent of the law."

After the Butte Flume and Lumber Company was taken over by Sierra Flume and Lumber Company in 1876, the new management placed in its book of general rules the following notice to its employees: "Superintendents will prevent all persons from riding down the flumes. Employees of the company will not be permitted to ride in any of the flumes, except to make repairs, or in case of emergency, where the business of the company requires someone to go quickly to the valley."[11]

Of course, attempts to forbid recreational use could not deny the convenience that the flume provided or the allure of excitement it presented. Just as today, people back then felt that some rules were meant to be broken,

Sketch of a man riding on a homemade boat on the flume from the Belle Mill to Sesma (Tehama County), although the steep cliffs are somewhat exaggerated. Drawn by Will L. Taylor, circa 1877. *Courtesy of CSU, Chico, Meriam Library, Special Collections. Donated by W.H. Hutchinson. Permission to reproduce granted by the California History Room, California State Library, Sacramento, California.*

and apparently this was one
of them. The flume was the
quickest way down to the
valley, a nice alternative to
the slow, bumpy ride down
a wagon road. People often
walked the narrow catwalks
on the high trestles to get
from one place to another
in a shorter amount of time
and with less effort or just to
get a good view.

There are many stories of
exciting rides in homemade
flume boats, a sensation of
adventure that could not be
matched anywhere else—
rushing down the watery
trough with water splashing
in your face while ducking
obstacles, such as protruding
rocks or overhanging
branches. If you happened
to make the trip during a
workday, there was always
a chance of running into a
lumber jam, maybe hard
enough to knock you off
your craft. Once you began
the ride, there was no

Women and children alike were fascinated by just
watching the water rush by. *Courtesy of CSU, Chico,
Meriam Library, Special Collections. Donated by Ruth
Hughes Hitchcock.*

turning back. You might be able to leave the main flow at infrequent water
diversion switches used by the flume tenders, which could be located miles
apart. Or maybe you could somehow stop the boat on a slow stretch of
water and take your chances with the narrow and often slippery planks used
as walkways. Although the flume builders tried to maintain a constant grade,
this was almost impossible to do, so nearly all flumes had varying slopes
along the way, with some stretches close to level and others dropping like a
playground slide.

A well-known Chico local named Paul Roberts, who wrote a regular
column for the *Chico Record* during 1947, described what he remembered

about the flume as a kid growing up near Sierra Lumber's Chico factory. Although this was during the waterway's final years, his account could probably be generalized to the entire time the flume was in operation:

> *There was something about the flume that thrilled you, the danger, the varying height, the speed of the water, the lumber floating down in an endless stream. Men, women and kids liked to climb the flume, walk the twelve inch plank along one side or ride a raft of lumber...We kids had fun swimming in the flume on Sundays when there was no lumber coming down.*
>
> *...On a good slope the water—and lumber—traveled up to 20 or 30 miles per hour...*
>
> *...The picknickers and thrill seekers walked this plank too, especially on Sundays and holidays, despite warning signs and the caretakers who tried to shoo us off. There were no speeding autos in those days but we humans were bitten by the thrill-bug just the same and naturally had to do something about it. So, the flume was our thriller.*[12]

A reporter visiting from San Francisco colorfully described his boat ride, which was guided by the superintendent of the flume, Mr. Hammil, from the Cascade Mill to Chico. A part of the account follows:

> *The flume stretched away until lost to sight, like a great sinuous serpent. Five miles from our starting point we came to Cape Horn. Here my conductor called out to me: "Hold on tight. We have come to a steep grade." As he spoke, the boat shot down with terrific velocity. Rocks, trees and scenery became a confused medley of whirling passing phantoms. A projecting piece of timber, the least break in the flume, and we would have been hurled to immediate death.*
>
> *...Passing under a projecting rock that threatened to sweep us from our seats, we dashed around the Devil's Elbow, a curve so abrupt that the forward end of the boat overleapt the side of the flume.*
>
> *...During this remarkable ride I felt no fear. The most dangerous places created no sensation beside that of awe. In many senses it was charming, delightful. It was more marvelous than Sinbad's flight on the back of the mystic roc.*
>
> *...The strain upon my nerves was intense; strung to their utmost tension, as I was hurled with inconceivable swiftness along to where Death beckoned, almost clutched me. They would suddenly relax as the boat found quiet level and I moved on softly as a zephyr. This constant, awful repetition of excitement and reaction left me at the journey's end weak and exhausted.*[13]

Early Logging in Northeastern California

The quote is part of a lengthy account given by the visiting newsman from the *San Francisco Post*. Corresponding to a Chico newspaper, the man from San Francisco claimed to have, at one point, traveled 2 miles in one minute. This would equate to 120 miles per hour, so the author believes he may have actually meant 1 mile in two minutes, which would have been more reasonable—that is, 30 miles per hour. The reporter also calculated a speed of almost 50 miles per hour at a point lower down, which was still fast but not unbelievable.

There are reports that other flumes existed, as well, that included steep grades with water rushing through with a high degree of swiftness. For instance, it's been written that Ellsworth's flume from the Belle Mill contained a stretch in which the water sped along at fifty miles per hour, while one near Carson City, Nevada, supposedly offered thrill seekers rides averaging about eighty miles per hour.

Sherman Reynolds took the same ride as the aforementioned reporter but started from the Arcade Mill, slightly downstream from the Cascade Mill. He was returning home to Chico after spending the summer near the mill and was given permission to make the trip by a relative, who had charge of the mill. A portion of his recollection of the experience is described below:

> *The first mile or two the scenery was just grand. The canyon in which the flume is situated is very narrow and deep, hence on my right and left hand almost perpendicular walls rose to an imposing height. As I was swept swiftly along I could not help shouting for ecstasy. But I soon had something else to think about. I rounded a sharp corner with such a jerk that I almost went out of the flume.*
>
> *From this time on there was no more scenery for me. All I could see was that flume and raft. I soon passed five or six sharp turns, and then saw the flume stretching away in front of me in an almost straight line; but, oh, my! how steep! The rate at which I cleared the next mile or two would have made a locomotive ashamed of itself. I had been warned about that place, so I was prepared; but at the end of the stretch I rounded a curve on a trestle ninety feet high. My blood blood [sic] ran cold, and as though to extend that same condition of temperature over my whole body, an abbreviated tidal wave of cold mountain water poured over the back end of my raft, soaking me to the skin. It is probably needless to say that I was not prepared for that.*
>
> *…I have thought this ride over a good many times and the more I think the firmer I am in my decision that I will come home next time by the road.*[14]

27

Of course, kids liked to get into the act too. Mrs. Nellie Weber recounted from her youth a time when she and two other young girls once attempted to board a makeshift raft for an exciting ride down a section of the flume. Upon boarding the little boat, it immediately sank into the cold water and submerged all three of them. When the young Weber and another girl managed to scramble out onto the walkway, the watercraft bobbed back to the surface, carrying the remaining passenger off into the distance. The lone rafter was rescued at the next flume station, and all three of the drenched girls were eventually reunited and treated to a warm fire from the flume attendant's kitchen stove. Their drenched garments were wrung out and dried before they returned home. What a fun day that was for the adventuresome young ladies.[15]

Of course, bad mishaps also occurred on flumes—Ellsworth's accident, for one. There is also a story about Will Bennet, who was killed by a projecting sliver while rounding a curve down the Blue Ridge flume on his way to Red Bluff to attend a Fourth of July celebration. Workers were at particular risk for death or injury. For instance, a seventy-foot-high trestle on the Flea Valley flume, south of Big Chico Creek, came down underneath four men who were trying to break a lumber jam, killing two of the workers.[16] Painful but not fatal injuries occurred too. On the Chico Creek flume, Johnny Wilson was trying to move lumber around with his hand when it got jammed. A part of one of his fingers was mashed so severely that a doctor had to take it off.

The Big Chico Creek flume itself was also subject to injury. Despite its impressive framework, Mother Nature sometimes felt it necessary to make a statement about the waterway's vulnerability to harsh weather conditions. One time, she received a little help from a lumber jam near what was at the time called the "Chinese Station." The jam caused a break in the flume, causing the water spill out and making it particularly susceptible to the high winds that ended up taking out thirty-two lengths of the structure.[17] Of course, Mother Nature didn't really need help from lumber jams, as evidenced one winter day in December 1879, when a severe storm blew through and simply knocked down the flume in many places.[18] General Bidwell had problems with his flume too. On more than one occasion, excessive water caused breaks in the structure and flooded parts of the town.[19]

The second major technological revolution to hit the northeastern California logging industry was introduced by a man named John Dolbeer. Like many others who immigrated to the West during the gold rush years, it was not long before Dolbeer realized that he was not going to be very successful at mining. Fortunately, he was able to fall back on a trade that he was already familiar with—logging. After working in the lumber industry for a time near the California coast, John accumulated enough money to become a founding partner in Dolbeer and Carson Lumber Company in Eureka. Dolbeer was a problem solver and inventor. At one time in his career, he worked as a naval engineer, and it was his experience with small steam engines used on ships that inspired him to invent a similar device to skid logs more easily to landings near coastal mills, thereby replacing the need for horses and oxen to do this same work. The little steam engine was commonly referred to as a "steam donkey" or "donkey engine" and was patented in 1882 as a "logging engine." The term "donkey" was used on ships because it was utilized as an auxiliary engine that did not possess the hauling power of a full-grown horse.

When Dolbeer's logging engine was patented, it was fairly simple in design and limited in its ability to haul heavy loads. An upright steam boiler powered an engine that turned a horizontal shaft with a small gear on it that meshed with a much larger gear attached to another horizontal shaft. Spools, called "gypsies," were mounted on both ends of this shaft, and at one corner in the front end of the donkey, rollers were attached to guide the rope into the winding gypsy, regardless of the angle from which the rope arrived at the rollers. (Snatch blocks could replace the rollers at either corner so that logs could be moved with either gypsy from any direction.)

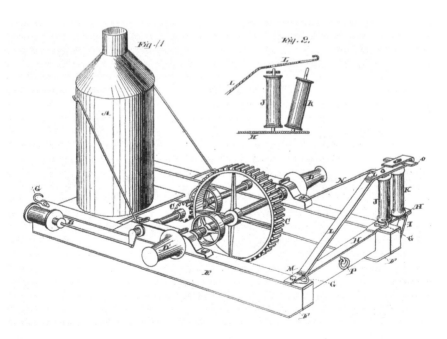

Dolbeer's "logging engine" patent, page 1. *Courtesy of U.S. Patent and Trademark Office.*

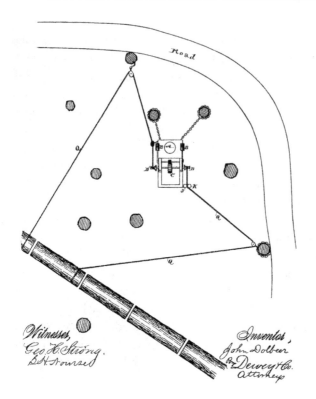

Dolbeer's "logging engine" patent, page 2. *Courtesy of U.S. Patent and Trademark Office.*

The machine was mounted on a strong frame, which could be anchored to stumps or trees by ropes or chains guided through eyebolts or hooks secured to the frame. The entire apparatus rested on "skids," or "sleds," allowing the donkey to drag itself around in the woods.

In the basic procedure for early donkey operations, a "line horse" would drag the rope or cable to a log into the woods, and the "choker setter" would noose the line around a log. Since the machine engineer, called a "donkey puncher," was often too far away to see the choker, a middleperson called a "whistle punk" was stationed in between. The whistle punk tugged on a line connected to the whistle on the engine when the log was ready to be pulled. (Sometimes flagmen relayed signals instead.) The donkey puncher would open the throttle, the donkey would start pulling and the "spool tender" then guided the incoming line over the spool with a stick. When a "haulback line" was added to the operation years later, the line horse was no longer needed.

One drawback to the donkey engine was the fact that it was fueled with wood and had a tendency to shower the crew with embers. Most of them could slap themselves to snuff out the fiery chunks of ash or simply take off their shirts. But not the spool tender, who had to diligently man his post the entire time the log was being reeled in—just hang in there and tough it out. As to be expected, donkey engines were known for starting a few forest fires.

Dolbeer's logging engine was quickly accepted in the woods east of the northern portion of the Sacramento Valley, first being used at Chico Meadows in 1886. The little steam engines could skid as many logs in one half hour as a bull team could in half a day. Over time, improvements made the donkey engine a much bigger, more powerful and more versatile machine. Steel cable replaced rope, and multiple drums that rotated on a horizontal plane took over for the little vertically spinning side spools. The early donkeys didn't even have a place to contain the leftover cable, so back then it was just coiled on the ground. At first, the yarding range of the donkey was limited to a few hundred feet, and ox teams generally took over from there to bring it the rest of the way to the landing. Eventually, however, the machines became so powerful that they could "road" logs hundreds of yards from one donkey to another along a skid road all the way to a mill. Steam donkeys not only became useful for "ground-lead" logging—that is, dragging logs along the forest floor—but they also performed many other functions too, such as loading railroad cars, hoisting up or lowering railroad cars through steep inclines and building trestles. They were even used to power wheels at the stern of steamboats.

With ground-lead logging operations, the timber that was being dragged around just crashed through debris, knocking down anything in the way, often picking up stones that might damage mill saws. The logs would frequently get hung up on stumps and rocks too.

In the early 1900s, the donkey made it possible to employ a more efficient and spectacular way to move logs around. "High-lead" logging employed daredevil climbers who would scale tall trees, sawing off limbs on the way up, until they reached a point twenty-five to thirty feet from the top, where they would cut off the crown. A heavy pulley block was then secured to the top of the decapitated tree, and guy wires were attached to the trunk in order to steady it against the mighty forces to which it would eventually be subjected. This "spar tree" could now serve as the support for a main line that was connected to logs lying on the ground. When the donkey engine was given the signal, one end of the log would be lifted up and pulled along by the lead cable, while its lower end jumped out of the brush like a giant jackrabbit. The logs would then be dumped into a pile with others. Yes, it's probably safe to say that Dolbeer's simple invention eventually became established as the little donkey that could do just about anything.

CHAPTER 2

WHEN THE WEST BRANCH MILL OPENED IN BIG CHICO CREEK CANYON

In 1878, the Sierra Lumber Company was incorporated to take over for the short-lived, often unpopular and bankrupt Sierra Flume and Lumber Company, which at one time was known as the most diverse lumber operation in the world, with its sawmills, planing mills, sash and door factories, retail yards, telegraph lines, tramways, flumes and wide range of office buildings making it a giant in the industry. The new company was initially under the control of some of the same individuals who helped run the previous one into the ground. (The financial panic in San Francisco and two years of drought in the valley didn't help.) However, an improving economic climate, sound practices and the hiring of solid managers made Sierra Lumber a successful company for many years to come.

Not long after it began the takeover, Sierra Lumber divided its operations into two divisions—Red Bluff and Chico. The Blue Ridge division was abolished, and most of its machinery and equipment was transferred to the Red Bluff division's Lyonsville area. The abandoned Blue Ridge flume was dismantled where possible, and some of the materials were used to build homes in the Manton area. In 1881, the terminus of the flume that followed Antelope Creek was moved from Sesma to the east bank of the river at Red Bluff, to the old Blue Ridge Flume and Lumber Company factory site. This facility would become the world's largest pine manufacturing plant by 1891 and California's second-largest sash and door factory. Unfortunately, the mighty Sacramento River had a tendency to flood the factory and its lumberyard on occasion, creating considerable downtime.

Early Logging in Northeastern California

During the two decades bracketing the turn of the twentieth century, foothill operations on the Red Bluff division were centered in the area surrounding the town of Lyonsville and the Champion Mill, which was now at the head of the flume that followed along Antelope Creek. The mill burned to the ground in 1891, but Sierra Lumber wasted no time in rebuilding it.[20] The Champion's narrow-gauge logging railroad, established in 1881, was apparently the first of its kind in the northern Sierra and originally used wooden rails faced with strap iron. It may be of interest to note that, at the time, there were no taxes levied on widths that were not commonly used in America, so this non-standard 39.35-inch width, known as European meter gauge, was exempt from that expense, at least initially. This first roadbed did not have trestles either, choosing to go the long route and snake its way around tight canyon heads instead. Some of the curves were so sharp that the trains were compelled to carry a giant screw jack as standard equipment, to put the locomotive back on the track. Eventually, the twisted little railroad track appeared to cover about twenty miles, and trestles were built to reduce some of the road's meandering ways.

The railroad had a highly publicized train wreck in 1901, the result of the "Big Waible" trestle collapsing underneath the weight of a logging train passing over it. Brakeman Jesse Bowen was riding one of the cars when it plunged into the ravine and was killed almost instantly. During the spectacular wreck, the two other cars and the locomotive were pulled into the ravine, and the engineer and fireman also suffered severe injuries. Lawsuits followed.[21] The Lyonsville rail operations had at least one other logging fatality around that same time. A brakeman, named Frank Doty, was killed when logs that had shifted on the car he was riding on crushed him. Apparently, the danger was so great that someone familiar with the situation was once quoted as casually saying, "If you got killed railroading at Lyonsville, why you just got killed, that's all."[22]

The Lyonsville railroad could also make claim to one of the most amazing escapes from certain death. Joseph Barker, a brakeman, fell between some moving cars. One of the wheels on a one-thousand-pound car ran completely over his chest. (Good thing it wasn't loaded.) Joseph must have been built like a rock because he didn't even break any bones or suffer internal injuries. He had a bright red mark across his chest where the flange of the wheel left its mark, and he was most certainly sore afterward. All things considered, though, Joseph got off real cheap.[23]

It seems Lyonsville had its share of occupational fatalities around the turn of the century. On two different occasions, Chico newspapers reported a man getting killed in the woods during operations that involved pulling logs with a donkey engine. One man was caught between a rope and a log, while the other was struck in the stomach by a forty-pound hook that had broken loose. There may have been other fatalities too.

The Chico factory was rebuilt in 1880 after the previous one burned to the ground during the time of transition from one company to the next. This new factory covered sixteen acres and specialized in fruit box and tray stock and more. In 1897, the company filled an order from a local Chinese company to make 150 boxes one foot wide, one foot deep and two feet long, designed to ship the bones of deceased Chinese back to their homeland. While the Chinese were exhuming the remains of their brethren buried in the Chico Cemetery, a crowd gathered every afternoon to witness what to them seemed like a bizarre event.[24]

After 1881, only one sawmill at a time operated in the foothills of the Chico division. When the "New Arcade Mill," located in Chico Meadows, ran out of trees to harvest, another large mill was constructed in Big Chico Creek Canyon in 1895, near the confluence of Big Chico Creek and Campbell

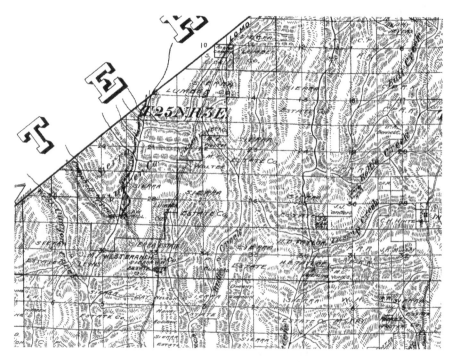

Official map of Butte County, 1901. Note the location of the sawmill and the road up to the ridge. A little logging railroad, extending from the mill to where it reached the Tehama County line, is also shown on the map. *Courtesy of Butte County Public Works.*

Creek. It was built on a large flat along Big Chico Creek, about a mile and a half from the West Branch stage stop that was located on the ridge above the creek, along the old Humboldt Wagon Road. The stop along the road had a hotel, a bar and a barn supplied with hay, oats and barley. It had been a popular resort destination for years.[25]

In 1864, John Bidwell and four partners incorporated the Chico and Humboldt Wagon Road, which wound its way from the valley in Chico to the eastern side of the Sierras at Susanville, Lassen County, not far from the Nevada border. The one-hundred-mile-long toll road was so named because its original purpose was to serve as a connection to the burgeoning silver mining industry in the Humboldt district of northwestern Nevada. By 1865, the road met with the Idaho Stage Company Line and offered Chico a way to tap into the rich silver mining operations of southwestern Idaho. Regular pack trains, wagons, stagecoaches and a mail contract showed promise of making Chico a major beneficiary of the commerce that the road was producing. However, the grand vision by Bidwell was plagued with problems, including harsh weather conditions, difficult terrain, competition from other roads and frequent Indian raids. With the completion of the transcontinental railway in 1869, it was evident that Bidwell's dream of a major supply route from Chico to Idaho had come to an end. However, the Humboldt Wagon Road would stay open for traffic to Susanville for many years to come, making the timber belt of the foothills much more accessible to the lumber industry. Communities sprang up along the way, teamsters hauled their freight and regular stages ran from Chico to Butte Meadows and Prattville, at one time or another. From Chico to Butte Meadows, regular stops along the road for water or rest included Hog Springs, Ten-Mile House, Fourteen-Mile House, Forest Ranch (Sixteen Mile-House), Berdan's, West Branch (on the ridge) and Lomo. The regular stage often left the Humboldt Road to make a side trip to the West Branch Mill also.

After over thirty years of heavy use, and by the time the West Branch Mill opened for business, the road was not what one might have described as "smooth sailing." On the contrary, it was very rough in many spots, and some of the grades were dangerously steep. In 1897, teamsters were known to refer to the Deadman and Lucas hills as "terrors."[26] The road had become so awful that there was even some thought about establishing a new thoroughfare from Chico to Forest Ranch through either Big Chico Creek Canyon or Little Chico Creek Canyon, the latter situated on the south side of the ridge. After creating a special commission to investigate the matter, the Chico Board of Trade was told that going through either canyon would be impractical, so they concluded that it would be best to make major repairs and reroute where necessary instead.[27] The road improvement project lasted longer than a year, with over one hundred individuals and businesses contributing in one way or another. New grades were made around six of the steepest hills.[28]

Unfortunately, not everyone took a liking to the new runarounds—Henry Addison certainly didn't. Henry owned some land between Berdan's and West Branch. He noted that the newly revised road went through part of his land, and he wanted the county to compensate him for it. When Henry's requests were ignored, the persistent landowner decided to take matters into his own hands. He dumped garbage on the road, felled trees across it and dug a trench through it. Of course, when you mess with the bull, you get the horn, and Henry's rebellious behavior did not go over very well with Mr. Bidwell and company. Henry was promptly arrested for his misguided ways. When Constable Chubbick brought the irritated man to Chico to face charges, a reporter for the *Chico Daily Record* found the situation kind of humorous. He described Henry's incarceration as such: "Addison was not in good humor; in fact he was so angry that he refused to accept the hospitality of the Constable and therefore went to bed with an empty stomach. He will probably be ready for breakfast this morning."[29]

Henry's defiance didn't get him very far. When his lawyer convinced him it just wasn't worth the effort to go against the road builders, the defeated property owner agreed to give them the deed to the land in dispute and not create any more obstructions. With these concessions, he was allowed to leave for home.[30]

After the road was improved, there were still problem spots. Starting immediately out of Chico, passengers were provided with a bone-jarring ride in many places along the way, as the road passed through a rocky volcanic mudflow called the Tuscan Formation, laid down in a layered sequence about three to four million years ago.

Sometimes Mother Nature just felt like adding more insult to injury. One time, between Berdan's and West Branch, the snow drifted so bad that the stage leaned way over and dumped all six of its passengers headfirst into the snow. Another time, the rains damaged the road down to the West Branch Mill severely enough that the stage company felt compelled to drop off mill passengers at the stage stop on the ridge instead. After an elderly lady destined for the mill had to walk the distance during a heavy rain, arriving at the mill thoroughly drenched, the stage company reevaluated the situation and arranged for a team of horses to transport people down. The County Seat Grade, below Ten-Mile House, had a rock overhang that posed a threat at all times and a treacherous curve where Al Silva, his daughter, their wagon and team (an old horse and a mule) all went over the edge of a steep drop-off. Al and his daughter were lucky to have survived the incident. Above Forest Ranch, the road was once so bad that the stage had to take to the woods in several places. It's no wonder that some people preferred to travel by lumber flume instead.

Returning to Sierra Lumber, a man named Bernard "Barney" Cussick supervised the building of the new mill in Big Chico Creek Canyon. At first, the site was simply referred to by the local papers as "Cussick's Mill" (not to be confused with his Smokey Creek Mill, near Deer Creek, which was a contract mill), but later it went on to be called the "Providence Mill" or "West Branch Mill." Sometimes it was referred to as simply the mill(s) at West Branch, which suggests that the mill and stage stop were often considered as one community. The little village surrounding the mill was made up of mostly shacks, houses, a company store, a butcher shop, a blacksmith shop and, for a time, a small hospital. Some families lived at the site all year long.

Barney Cussick became Sierra Lumber's Chico division mountain manager in 1884, after contracting with the company for several years

West Branch Mill, circa 1903–04. Note what appears to be a steep road in the background, most likely the way to the stage stop. *From the Harris Moak collection. Courtesy of Dale Wangberg.*

Another view of the West Branch Mill, circa 1902. Note the flumes near the stacks of lumber. *Courtesy of CSU, Chico, Meriam Library, Special Collections. Donated by Fred Young.*

previous.[31] He was managing the New Arcade Mill when he turned his attention toward developing the West Branch site. (It appears that by then he was no longer operating the Smoky Creek Mill.) The man made quite a name for himself over the course of his lifetime. During his illustrious logging career, Barney always tried to stay a step ahead. For instance, he was the first to use Dolbeer donkey engines and steam-hoisting equipment for logging in the Sierra. Soon after the completion of the mill in the Big Chico Creek Canyon, Barney resigned from Sierra Lumber in the summer of 1895 due to poor health and handed over the reins to his brother John.[32] It wasn't long before Barney found a new way to become successful—real estate. He was possibly best known during that stage of his life for subdividing a large part of John Bidwell's huge landholdings and developing the Chico orchard district. (The news reported that after moving his logging operations from Tehama to Butte County, closer to Chico, Barney jokingly said that his new mill was now in "Bidwell" County, perhaps giving a hint about his intentions for a career in Chico real estate.)[33] He was also instrumental in the development of Hamilton City and its sugar industry.[34] Barney became a prominent banker, and it was said that he was a member of what was jokingly referred to as the "Second Street Gang." These guys handled big business deals and probably controlled some of the politics, but they were also known for being honest men. Even though Barney was very instrumental in the business development of Butte County, we have only the naming of Cussick Avenue, in Chico, to honor him with today.

Barney was popular with just about everyone, made many friends and was always known for treating his employees very well, including giving them a snort of good whiskey when called for. As a result, it's been said the men worked hard for the man they affectionately called "Old Sugarfoot." After he retired from Sierra Lumber, Barney personally operated the "ambulance" that, when flume travel wasn't practical, rushed up to the mountains from the valley to rescue injured workers or expectant mothers and bring them down to civilization as quickly as possible, with his well-kept, fine horses and rigs. Barney supposedly did this for anyone, regardless of whether he knew them or not, and he didn't charge anything.

The Chico local, referred to earlier, who wrote a regular column for the *Chico Record*, fondly remembered the distinguished citizen as such:

> *Barney accumulated considerable cash in the log contracting business and then retired to Chico, where he accumulated more—and considerable avoirdupois. As a newsboy back there about 45 years ago I can still see Barney with his derby hat, big cigar and almost invariably dressed in a dark suit with perpendicular pin stripes which were supposed to make him look slender—but didn't!*[35]

As mentioned earlier, John "Jack" Cussick, one of Barney's two brothers, took over as superintendent of the mill in the canyon during the summer of 1895. He retained the job until December 1900, when he decided to pursue a more lucrative position with another lumber company located near the town of Sisson (the name was changed to Mount Shasta in 1924), in Siskiyou County. Like his brother Barney, John was a longtime employee of Sierra Lumber (twenty-one years) before leaving for greener pastures. His Sierra Lumber superiors were very satisfied with his stay at the helm also, and it was felt at the time that it would be difficult to fill his shoes. For his part, John stated upon his resignation that he was departing from the company that had treated him so well over the years with some feelings of regret. In addition to becoming the superintendent of the Wood & Sheldon Mill and being in charge of logging camps, he also purchased an interest in the new company.[36] John just happened to be the son-in-law of James McGann,

This photo was taken around 1902, when John Cussick was superintendent of the Wood & Sheldon Mill, in Siskiyou County, California. *Courtesy of Perry Sims.*

the man who compiled the official Butte County maps of 1877 and 1886,[37] which included the route of the Chico Creek flume.

John Cussick eventually left Wood & Sheldon, in 1909, to work as manager of the woods and sawmill at Lyonsville, although by then it was no longer Sierra Lumber Company. Diamond Match, a company whose roots were developed on the East Coast, bought out Sierra Lumber in 1907. Diamond actually began its California logging experience back in 1901, when there was an attempt by a man called Fredrick Deakin, who secured an option on the Chico division of Sierra Lumber, to sell the properties to Diamond. The Chico division deal didn't materialize. However, Deakin managed to sell Diamond forty thousand acres of timberland, covering three counties, called the Sierra Estate. After purchasing the original acreage from Deakin, Diamond added several more land acquisitions over the next two years, and who should handle the Chico real estate transfer but none other than Barney Cussick.

At that time, Diamond felt that fluming lumber was not its cup of tea, so it instead decided to build a railroad to move lumber down from the timber belt to the valley below. Before that, however, it had to decide where to put the upper sawmill. It chose a point on the Magalia Ridge, which it eventually named Stirling City. When the site for the valley remanufacturing plant was chosen, in Chico, the new company was ready to roll. In early 1903, work began on the Stirling City mill, the valley mill (at a site referred to as Barber) and the Butte County Railroad. Before lumber was hauled on the line, the railroad provided regular passenger service between Barber and Magalia in late 1903. The railroad to Stirling City was not completed until early 1904, when it was able to deliver much-needed machinery to the mill. By the time the Stirling City mill was ready to go, it had plenty of logs stored in its mill pond from timber that was accessed via spur tracks from the railroad line to company-owned land. In 1905, Diamond enjoyed its first full season of operation. Early on, the growing Southern Pacific Railroad took ownership of the Butte County Railroad, although a deal was made so that Diamond could lease it back. (Southern Pacific had also taken charge of the California and Oregon Railroad at some time.)

The Butte County Railroad had a highly publicized death near Stirling City in 1906. Conductor Lautenschlager, along with two others, was sitting at the head of a loaded log car that was in the front of a slow-moving train descending a hill when the car's lead trucks derailed. All of the riders leapt for safety, but somehow the conductor tripped and fell underneath the wheels.

When John Cussick left Wood & Shelton, in 1909, to work for Diamond Match at Lyonsville, he replaced a man called Frank Thatcher. Ironically, it was Frank who had succeeded John as superintendent of the West Branch Mill, back in 1900.

So began a new era in the West Branch family of loggers and millworkers, with Frank M. Thatcher taking on the role as the new boss of the lumber operations in Big Chico Creek Canyon. Frank was another person who was known for being smart, energetic, dedicated and popular with those he worked with. He started working as a young man for Sierra Lumber in the mid-1880s. One source suggested he started by packing mules and horses for construction work on tramways before getting a job packing horses with two twenty-gallon bags of water for domestic use in camps and fueling donkey engines. Another indicated he began as a fireman in one of the hoisting stations. Either way, Frank quickly worked his way up the ladder to get to the top position he eventually earned at the West Branch Mill.[38] Not only did he stay with the West Branch Mill through to its final days, but he continued on with Diamond Match after it had taken over Sierra Lumber. With Diamond, Frank went on to have a very successful career in logging, heading the Stirling City operations for many years. Among other things, he initiated the use of high-lead logging.

Frank Thatcher, from Mansfield's 1918 book *History of Butte County.*

While working for Diamond one day in 1910, Frank demonstrated his bravery in a most spectacular way. It seems that he was hosting an excursion train near Stirling City, with fifteen guests riding on a flat car that was positioned behind a locomotive and three cars loaded with logs. They were moving smoothly along when the little train approached a 4.5 percent grade and began to accelerate swiftly. When it became evident that the little engine could not control the runaway train any longer and the trainmen couldn't reach hand brakes that were blocked by logs, the entire train crew jumped. Then, to save his guests from a gruesome end, the quick-thinking superintendent sprang into action. One of the party members, a teacher from Chico, described the harrowing incident as follows:

> I never had such a wild ride in my life. We fairly flew along the road. Trees dashed by with lightning like rapidity.
>
> I did not realize that anything was wrong and thought that we were just making time until Mr. Thatcher with a ring of terror in his voice shouted to us to hold tight and not jump.
>
> Then I noticed how terribly fast we were going. Men were tumbling off the front of the train and rolling in the dust as we swept by. Mr. Thatcher was the hero and if he hadn't crept up in front of the swaying car and uncoupled it I'm sure some of us would have been killed. He hung on to the brake and twisted it with grim determination. Slowly, slowly the car commenced to slow down. Just ahead of us the train was tearing madly down the grade. Then there was this crash, the two engines had collided with a deafening roar. It was exciting while it lasted, but I don't want another such experience. The men told us after it was all over that we women behaved admirably. I guess it was because we were too scared to do anything else.[39]

Thatcher was eventually thrown from the car into a ditch. When picked up, he was bruised and shaken and had an injured knee. The engine and three log cars continued down the steep slope and ultimately slammed into a standing train, causing considerable damage to the equipment.

CHAPTER 3

OBSTACLES AND ACCOMPLISHMENTS

The West Branch Mill had a little railroad of its own, built when the harvestable trees nearby began to run out and the lumber company desired to reach out farther into the woods to feed the mill. For a distance of about two miles downstream from the mill, the gentle terrain bordering the edges of the creek was quite accommodating for pulling logs along chutes placed on the ground or maybe even using big-wheeled log carts. Transporting logs from above the mill, however, was more challenging because it required negotiating through steep walls of the canyon that extended right down to the creek while crossing several deep gorges that were carved out by feeder creeks. Here, the railroad would provide a much quicker way than chutes to road the logs back to the mill. In August 1899, a fifteen-ton narrow gauge locomotive arrived in Chico to be transported to the West Branch Mill. At that time, the newly constructed track extended upstream about two and a half miles, but plans to extend it followed soon afterward.[40] This little logging railroad, running on thirty-pound rail, was reported to be the first of its kind in Butte County.

Narrow gauge was probably chosen for several reasons. For one thing, it was more appropriate for the confined, curvy canyon that, recall, at one time was considered even too rugged for a lumber flume. Narrow gauge was also cheaper to build.

The little railroad eventually added another engine to its roster, so that two 0-6-0T "tank" locomotives operated around the mill. Tank locomotives, in general—some may be familiar with the *Thomas the Tank Engine* book and television series—were manufactured primarily for industrial application

Train crossing a trestle in Big Chico Creek Canyon, taking logs back to the mill. Note the brakemen spread out along the train. *Courtesy of CSU, Chico, Meriam Library, Special Collections. Donated by Fred Young.*

Sometimes trains would transport workers. *Courtesy of CSU, Chico, Meriam Library, Special Collections. Donated by Glenn Dietz.*

and saw limited use on the mainline. These engines did not require that a tender be hauled behind, as they were built to carry their own fuel (wood, oil or coal) and water. This allowed the locomotives to move easily back and forth. This kind of engine was well suited for running in areas of restricted space, such as in the steep, narrow canyon surrounding Big Chico Creek.

The particular type of locomotive used on the West Branch Mill railroad line was referred to as a "saddle tanker." This was because the water tank was positioned above the boiler, fitting over it like a saddle, which provided more weight for traction and naturally preheated the water. The trade-off was that the engineer's vision may have been more restricted. Furthermore, the little locomotives used in Big Chico Creek Canyon were limited in their power to push or pull cars, and they only had a lever brake and a steam jam to slow them down.

There is not much information available in regard to the other equipment used by the little railroad, but by piecing together historic photos and what little documentation still exists, a general description can be developed. The

No. 1, used in Big Chico Creek Canyon, circa 1904. Charles Marion is in the cab. His son, Harry, is leaning against the bunker that appears to be filled with wood for fuel. The 0-6-0T engine had three drive axles (six wheels) but no pilot or trailing axles. Note how the water tank rests on the boiler like a saddle. *Courtesy of CSU, Chico, Meriam Library, Special Collections. Donated by Glenn Dietz.*

logs were hauled on two four-wheeled trucks, connected by a narrow bar in between. Each truck was fitted with a bunk to rest the timbers, which were secured to the trucks with chains. Although these cheap and easy-to-build trucks were versatile pieces of equipment that were well suited for operations like those in Big Chico Creek Canyon, one drawback was that the cars would have a tendency to buckle when shoving a number of empties uphill, like up a steep spur track. Another problem was that this kind of railroad operation did not allow the use of air brakes that could be controlled throughout the train by the engineer, although the little saddle tankers didn't have anything to accommodate this mode of slowing down the train anyway. Therefore, brakemen often had the dangerous job of controlling the downhill speed of the train by riding the cars and applying individual hand brakes on the move. If the train was going slow enough, the trainman could hop from car to car to manipulate more than one hand brake. However, if the speed was too fast, he was forced to travel over the swaying logs as if he was part of a high-wire balancing act.

The West Branch Mill railroad also appeared to utilize "slab" cars. Sierra Lumber records suggest these rail cars were used around the canyon to deliver, probably among other things, cooking supplies to the logging camps.[41] Unfortunately, documentation in regard to all of the rolling stock used on the little railroad is difficult to locate, possibly because the San Francisco fire from the 1906 earthquake destroyed much of Sierra Lumber's records.

The railroad in Big Chico Creek Canyon used the "link-and-pin" system for connecting cars to each other and to the locomotive. Link-and-pin were the original type of couplers used on railroads in America, but logging lines continued to use them even after the more advanced knuckle coupler was introduced. This was because the link-and-pin was simpler to use and the parts were easier to make in the mill's blacksmith shops. Link-and-pin connections were also less likely than knuckles to have an unexpected uncoupling on rough and uneven track. When an overhanging log would make it difficult to hook up the cars directly with a typical link, the system could easily accommodate longer connectors, called "roosters." Compared to the couplers in use today, the link-and-pin system was a slow and dangerous way to connect cars. The trainman had to stand between the moving cars while they were coming together in order to guide the link into the drawbar. Quite a few men working on railroad lines with this kind of equipment were injured or killed over the years because they could not get their limbs or bodies out of the way in time. After stopping, the pin was inserted into the top of the drawbar to secure the connection.

Early Logging in Northeastern California

This link-and-pin coupling can be seen on a train operating on Sierra Lumber's "other" division, near Lyonsville. Although there were many different types of link-and-pin coupler systems in use, the ones in Big Chico Creek Canyon may have been similar to this. *Courtesy of CSU, Chico, Meriam Library, Special Collections.*

As it was, the terrain made it difficult to build the roadbed. It's truly a wonder the lumber company was able to build a series of strong trestles that spanned across the wide and constantly eroding gorges with so little ground that could be considered solid support. Like the flume, it was an amazing technological feat. As the years went by, Sierra Lumber would simply extend the railroad when the available timber became depleted. By 1902, it was reported that the railroad snaked along Big Chico Creek about six miles upstream from the mill. In 1904, reports indicated that more track was added, although how much, and where, was not specified.[42]

A large part of the main track was on a very gentle slope. The one relatively steep part was about a two-mile stretch, with an average grade of around 4 percent—located between the first trestle above the mill to cross Big Chico Creek and the trestle that crossed Big Bear Creek. However, the spur that followed Little Smokey Creek was quite a bit steeper, with a grade that averaged about 7 to 8 percent. This was too steep to allow a little locomotive coupled up to a heavy load of logs to control its speed downhill. Therefore,

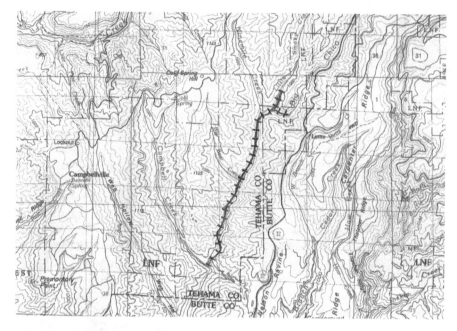

The sketch, drawn by the author and superimposed on a TOPO! software map, is an approximation of the route the West Branch Mill railroad tracks followed, to the best of the author's knowledge. It does not show the numerous small bends that were made in order to negotiate through the feeder streams in the winding canyon. *Appreciation to the* National Geographic *maps division for allowing the contour map to be reproduced.*

it's likely that the little engine shoved three or four empty cars up the track, cut away from them and then went back down the hill by itself. The loaded cars would then be rolled back down the hill by brakemen, usually one to a car, who controlled the speed with hand brakes—a common practice on steep spurs. When several cars were rolled down together, it was always hoped that a frightened trainman would not abandon his post (some refer to this as "joining the birds"), leaving the others dangerously shorthanded at a most critical time.

After the West Branch Mill opened, there was no longer a need for the lumber flume above this point, since Sierra Lumber only operated one mountain mill at a time in the Chico division. Therefore, the upper section of the flume was abandoned and a link was made that connected the new mill to the remainder of the flume, at a point just below Campbell Creek. The thirty-seven-mile-long flume was now a twenty-five-mile-long flume.

The mill sliced up mostly sugar pine, the preferred wood, and some ponderosa pine (also known as yellow pine today but apparently referred to as white pine in the early days of logging). However, it's also been reported that fir was cut for construction use and for flume building and repair. The mill generally produced about eleven million feet of lumber annually. Sugar pine, known as the world's largest pine, and which has been referred to as the "king of pines," can soar up to over two hundred feet above the ground, with a trunk diameter of seven feet, or even larger on occasion. Its impressive cones can grow one and a half feet long and a half foot wide, the largest of any conifer. Some individuals have been known to live over five hundred years. It was the most sought-after wood at the time of the West Branch Mill, and today it is still a major lumber species, despite the fact that it rarely grows in pure stands anymore and is usually scattered throughout mixed coniferous forests instead. The light, durable wood that is resistant to changes in humidity is an excellent material in house construction, especially for making shakes, window sashes and doors. The settlers used the lumber for constructing bridges and flumes, and miners used it as mine timbers. Once the wood dried, it left no scent, so it was also popular for making fruit and vegetable crates. Ponderosa pine is the most common and widely distributed western conifer and occurs mostly in pure stands. Although not known as the king, it, too, can grow to be a very large tree with high commercial value for making window frames and panel doors. After drying, ponderosa pine also resists expanding and shrinking with weather conditions, so it is used for many other applications, as well.

Like most mills in the foothills, the West Branch operations were seasonal because the snow and rain would eventually make the ground too soft to work in, usually by November. Operations would then resume sometime in the spring, around April or May. The mill generally employed between 150 and 200 men during the summer months,[43] with most of them returning to the valley when it shut down for the winter. The rest stayed behind to build chutes, do repair work, overhaul equipment and make other preparations for the upcoming season.

The West Branch Mill had a reputation for its innovative, sometimes unique, operations. For instance, at the time, it was one of a small number of mills in northern California to make use of a log pond. As early as 1896, local newspapers were printing reports from visitors who were amazed at the mill's machinery and multifaceted operations in the woods and its magnificent execution of tree harvesting. One account indicated that the mill had already built about ten miles of main chutes and branches and marveled at how the logs "shot down the chutes" before dumping into the pond. Even more impressive to these visitors was seeing the donkey engines pulling down trees from eighteen inches to two feet in diameter.[44] About a month later, another group of people were touring

Above: The West Branch Mill was one of only a few mills in northern California at that time to make use of a log pond. *Courtesy of CSU, Chico, Meriam Library, Special Collections. Donated by Glenn Dietz.*

Left: The photo shows a string of logs waiting to splash into the West Branch Mill log pond. This appears be the same structure that can be seen in the background on the left-hand side of the previous photo. *Courtesy of Bancroft Library University of California, Berkeley.*

the Humboldt Wagon Road from Chico to Prattville. Along the way, they dropped down to the mill site and were also captivated: "The scenery at that point is absolutely grand—the turbulent stream, the busy mill, and the splash of the logs as they dropped into the stream, only to be grappled and drawn up to the saw, to be transformed into lumber. It was indeed a grand sight."[45]

In 1902, Deputy Fish Comissioner L.N. Kircheval visited the mill and told others that he had never seen one that operated so systematically or showed as much production in

This log is being pulled from the pond to be fed to the saws. This is the same ramp that can be seen in the photo on page 50, except from the opposite side. *Courtesy of Bancroft Library University of California, Berkeley.*

proportion to the number of men working. For slicing up the lumber, the mill used what was called a "double circular" saw. In 1900, Charles "Biddy" Williams became the head sawyer for the mill and carried a strong reputation with him for excellence. Biddy's work ethic, starting as a dishwasher and then working in just about every department of the mill, brought him up through the ranks to eventually attain the position of prominence, operating boss of the mill, which he held for years.

Not that the record of the mill went completely unblemished. Sierra Lumber was once caught in the middle of a publicly exposed environmental controversy, when Kircheval investigated some local sawmills for allowing sawdust to get into streams, causing the death of fish. W.B. Dean, superintendent of Sierra Lumber at that time, flatly denied any wrongdoing and admonished the press for their direct accusation of the West Branch Mill specifically. After the inspection of a number of lumber mills, the deputy fish commissioner admitted that there were a few instances of neglect, but the problem was being corrected. He never mentioned to the press who the violators were.[46] Ironically, this occurred about around the same time period as his visit, referred to above, when he had nothing but high praises for the West Branch lumber operations.

In 1900, it was reported that Sierra Lumber Company paid out more money for labor than any other industry in Butte County, primarily because of the West Branch Mill. The Sierra Lumber Company not only employed a large number of people in the foothills, but the Chico planing mill and box factory it serviced with the now twenty-five-mile-long flume also employed about eighty more, full time. In addition to the two large foothill mills, the box factory in Chico and a sash and door plant in Red Bluff, Sierra Lumber also had branch yards in other parts of the state. This provided quite a network for the sites to share materials, so the Chico yard had plenty of windows and doors for sale. The Chico plant was also a sight to see, with its planers, edger, cut-offs, re-saw machines and a printing plant to label boxes. Furthermore, at one time it boasted the most modern equipment to remove waste materials to an outside dumping ground for others to collect. The locals would pick up kindling blocks for a nominal price, while the Chico Water Company collected the sawdust to use as fuel.[47]

Talking about one man's trash being another man's treasure, Sierra Lumber didn't see any value in the big cones that the fallen sugar pines left behind, but James Dodge sure did. The enterprising local, who lived nearby and was the overseer for the upper division of the Humboldt Wagon Road, made a profitable business by harvesting the material left behind by the West Branch loggers. James would collect the large strobili and sell them to people out of state. Not one to let an opportunity slip by, he would also mark the spots where white lilies and other sought-after flowers were located in the summertime and then come back in the fall to collect the bulbs. These were sold to dealers out of state too.[48]

Over the years, the West Branch Mill had to face numerous obstacles that would occasionally interfere with lumber production, like the equipment breaking down. However, winter storms probably caused the greatest amount of damage requiring repair work, especially to chutes, bridges and roads. The weather in 1904 proved to be especially troublesome for Sierra Lumber in Big Chico Creek Canyon. In February, it was reported in a local paper that an eighty-foot-high railroad trestle over Big Chico Creek, located about a quarter mile above the mill, was demolished due to heavy rain and would have to be totally rebuilt, which would surely delay the opening of the logging season. Fortunately, it was later reported that it was actually a smaller trestle that was washed out, and the interruption to work was not going to be nearly as bad as first thought.[49] However, just when the workers (many of whom had moved up with their families from their winter homes in the valley) had thought operations were ready to commence, a late April snowstorm struck the canyon with up to a foot of snow, delaying the start of the logging season once more. After everything that happened that winter and spring, it was determined that the storms had delayed the start of the season by about a month, compared to when it opened the previous year.[50] Even after all of that, the weather of 1904 was still not done with the lumbermen in Big Chico Creek Canyon. That same year, unusually heavy rains for October suspended operations before the company was ready to quit for the season, causing major damage to some roadways and forcing the company to deliver fresh supplies to some of the upper camps with packhorses.[51] The winter of 1906 was also hard on equipment and operations. It inflicted considerable damage to about 1,500 feet of track on the little railroad and knocked out part of the dam at the mill.[52]

As to be expected, wildfires were a major concern for the lumbermen. One year, a fire raging through the foothills came dangerously close to the mill, and the men worked late into the night to battle the blaze. That same day a fire also threatened the flume near China Switch station, lower downstream, but luckily, it was spared any damage. Not surprisingly, a donkey engine reportedly started at least one substantial fire, near the little settlement of Lomo. Again, employees of Sierra Lumber were called upon to get the flames under control, and this time they worked until the next morning. At one point, Lomo was in great danger of being destroyed, along with a large amount of Sierra Lumber property, but a sudden change in wind direction provided what the newspaper described as "an almost providential escape."[53] Just when the lumber boys thought they could relax, another fire broke out two days later, near Lomo again, and company workers were called out once more to suppress the flames and protect Sierra Lumber property. That one was presumably blamed on hot coals left in a campfire. The flume near China Switch was threatened on one other occasion, and the employees of the lumber company were called upon to protect it also. That time, arson was suspected.[54]

The "Palace," a flume tender station located in the canyon below Forest Ranch, burned to the ground one morning. Thankfully, Richard Price, his wife and several small children managed to escape the flames unharmed. The family hurried out so quickly that only one personal item was saved from the inferno—a sewing machine.[55]

The woods weren't the only places Sierra Lumber had to worry about fire. The Chico planing mill and box factory caught fire twice within six months of one another. The first blaze occurred in November 1903, and the cause was undetermined. The factory, engine house and dry houses were totally destroyed. The company lost about $40,000 worth of property, but it was only insured for $16,000. Luckily, rain from the previous day dampened the lumber in the yard, so most of it was saved. However, a lack of available water to fight such a large fire allowed the flames to spread relentlessly through buildings while helpless firemen stood by and watched. The manager of the mill made plans to immediately set up a temporary mill to handle what business it could, but arrangements were made to have the Red Bluff plant fill out contracts and ship what it could. As a result of the blaze, many local people were temporarily placed out of work, including those who depended on lumber materials to ply their trade, such as construction workers.[56] Needless to say, the ripple effect likely impacted the West Branch Mill.

Another crippling fire occurred in the spring of 1904, as if that wasn't already a bad enough year for Sierra Lumber. This inferno consumed about ten acres of the Chico yard, which took the brunt of the blaze. It was estimated that about ten million feet of stored lumber was lost and that the total cost, including the loss of equipment, materials and small buildings, was about $200,000, about twice as much as would be covered by insurance. Flames also threatened the newly built mill, but it was saved by an automatic internal sprinkler system. Although the mill building survived, the machinery within was flooded with water and required overhauling. However, Sierra Lumber wasn't the only one to suffer losses, as the flames also spread to

Spectators observing the 1904 fire at Sierra Lumber's Chico plant. *Courtesy of CSU, Chico, Meriam Library, Special Collections.*

nearby buildings and residences, burning some of these to the ground. Some people were frantically removing furniture and other belongings to safer locations, often with no need for alarm. One of the mill warehouses under siege contained two thousand pounds of dynamite destined for the West Branch Mill. (Although it could be pretty destructive at times, dynamite was sometimes used for splitting logs.) After being notified of this fact, the crowd watching the spectacle did not hesitate to run for cover and await an explosion. Luckily, the powder burned without incident. About $1,000 of groceries and supplies for the West Branch Mill was also lost in the inferno. This time, the flume was put to use in order to help fight the blaze. A sump hole was dug and filled with water from the waterway, which was able to supply three streams of water for dousing the lumber piles. It was believed that a spark from a yard locomotive or a Chinese cigarette probably started the fire.[57] In less than a week, the flume was repaired and ready to bring down lumber from the foothills once more.

Money destined for the West Branch Mill was also at risk. On one occasion, a stage destined for West Branch was robbed about a half mile above Hog Springs, along the Humboldt Wagon Road. Bob Cole, the driver, was compelled to stop when instructed to do so by a man hiding behind a rock fence, brandishing a double-barreled shotgun. The male passengers were then ordered to get out of the stage, while the lone female was allowed to stay inside. One of the passengers, however, got out on the opposite side of the stage that the inexperienced robber was facing and took the opportunity to empty the contents of his purse into his pockets before he was told to line up with the others. So, when the robber told the passengers to put their purses into a hat, the one with a little foresight contributed nothing to the bandit's cause but an empty purse. Cole was then instructed by the robber to throw out the express box (a container for safeguarding valuable items), but the driver had to explain to the uninformed hold-up man that the stage was not an express. After the stage was allowed to leave and the authorities arrived to inspect the crime scene, it was determined by footprints that there were actually two criminals involved. The robbers didn't even ask the driver to hand over what he had on his person, which was about eighty dollars, some of which was destined for the West Branch Mill. All told, the two inept bandits managed to get away with about four or five dollars.[58]

Another time, William Look was driving the stage to the West Branch Mill, with $600 in gold on board for Frank Thatcher, the mill superintendent. The driver put the coin in a sack and just tossed it in with the rest of the freight but in a place where he could keep an eye on it from his seat. Along the way, the stage stopped at several places to deliver packages, which required Look to go to the rear of the vehicle in order to retrieve them. When he returned to his seat after each delivery, William observed that the sack appeared to be undisturbed. But, when the stage arrived at the mills, it was discovered that about $155 was missing. Suspicion was immediately placed on one of the passengers, an elderly Oriental man who was to be employed at the mill. Look, who also served as a deputy constable, charged the man with having stolen the money, but the passenger flatly denied any wrongdoing. The deputy constable was not satisfied, however, so he searched the man and found the missing money. The accused then admitted that on one occasion when the stage driver was at the back of the stage, he slyly untied the string around the top of the sack, removed a few twenties and then put things back in their proper place.[59]

Sierra Lumber was once involved in reporting a holdup, although it wasn't the victim. One afternoon, two men robbed John Hollenbeck, an old gentleman over seventy years of age, who ran a small wayside station at Ten-Mile House along the Humboldt Road. Mr. Hollenbeck made a

This flume station was located in the canyon northwest of the Ten-Mile House location, on the ridge, and is believed to be the Rocky Point flume tender station. *Courtesy of CSU, Chico, Meriam Library, Special Collections. Donated by John Nopel.*

lucrative little business by selling tobacco, cigars and light refreshments, and the robbers probably heard that the old man kept a large sum of money around. James Garland, a teamster, happened upon the holdup and was also robbed. After the bandits fled the crime scene with Hollenbeck's horse and cart, Garland went down the trail into the canyon to report the crime on the Sierra Lumber telephone at the China Switch flume tender station.[60] (Since phones installed at the flume tender stations were sometimes the only ones available for miles around, they were often used to report non-company events, such as injuries or deaths.)

It may be interesting to note that, in 1895, the *Chico Enterprise* reported that there was not a well, nor any springs, near Ten-Mile House, so water was hauled up in barrels from the canyon below and sold to the road travelers. It was believed at the time that this was probably the only place in northern California where water was sold.[61] It seems that Ten-Mile House may have been a little ahead of its time.

Then there were those minor inconveniences with spooky equines, like the time when some of the West Branch Mill boys were traveling down to Chico on the stage and it stopped at Hog Springs for some water. When the lead horses became startled by the sound of one of the singletrees rubbing against the tin tank, they bolted with the empty carriage, leaving the driver and passengers stranded. About a half mile down the road, three of the frightened beasts managed to break away from the stage, which was by then a total wreck. The lumbermen had to walk to town from there, with their baggage left strewn about the road.[62] In those days, you didn't only have to be concerned with your vehicle possibly breaking down. You had to worry about it running away from you too.

Spooky horses could simply be a risk to your health. One of the men who drove horse-drawn cars from the Chico lumberyard to the California and Oregon mainline, located about a mile away, was a well-known former Indian fighter by the name of Simeon Moak. It's been said that Sim would carry a handful of rocks with him to remind the horses that resting was not an option.

Little did Sim know, but revenge was in the making. One time, a horse in the company stable kicked Sim in the side, launching him into the air for a distance of about eight feet before the side of the barn abruptly ended the flight. He was literally knocked out of work for a few days. However, his next encounter with an angry horse, about a year later, appeared to have resulted in even more severe injuries. No one near the scene, not even Sim himself, knew exactly how he was injured, although a few men working in the yard observed him approaching the horse, which was tied to a car. After that, all they could see was a cloud of dust and hear the rattling of chains. Simeon came out of the skirmish with four teeth missing, along with a part of his jawbone, two mashed toes and an assortment of bruises.[63]

As we've seen before, sometimes citizens of Chico could be a headache for Sierra Lumber. After finally securing permission to lay a railroad down on Ninth Street from the Chico mill to the mainline, the lumber company was still only allowed to use horses or mules to haul the freight along the track. Apparently, the property owners along Ninth Street were extremely opposed to a "steam horse" running through their neighborhood, presumably because of the smoke, dust and noise it would create. Finally, in late 1901, after a heated battle, Sierra Lumber was finally given permission to allow a steam locomotive to move the cars down Ninth Street.[64]

Cows could be an annoyance also. The train operators on the little railroad down in the canyon even had to be on the lookout for range cattle. One time, a logging train was traveling over a section of track that would not allow it to slow down enough to avoid running into bovines on the loose. One cow was killed, and several others were injured. The stockmen were told by Sierra Lumber that they had better move their cattle away from that area because the company was not going to be held accountable.[65] Sierra Lumber was just trying to offer some sound advice. When it comes to locomotive versus cow, it's no contest.

CHAPTER 4
UNFORTUNATE ACCIDENTS AND NARROW ESCAPES

While the Sierra Lumber Company in Big Chico Creek Canyon was operating between the years 1895 and 1906, danger was always present, and workers were injured on a regular basis, with some of the men becoming repeat offenders. Eventually, a hospital was opened at the mill site (more on that later), but many of the injured men were taken to Chico, by flume or over the wagon road, to receive treatment and recover from their injuries at boardinghouses, such as the Hallam House, Johnson House or Union Hotel. The Chico Sanitarium was another likely destination. Then again, some of the less injured employees elected to just stay in the hills during their recovery period, often because the temperature was more comfortable than the stifling heat the valley had to offer during the summer months.

It may be of interest to note that the anti-Chinese sentiment was quite obvious in at least two of these boardinghouses during this period. At one time or another, the Hallam House and the Johnson House advertised that they employed white labor only. One newspaper referred to the Johnson House and wrote: "In no department of the hotel has a Chinaman a place."[66] The Anti-Chinese League was having meetings, and newspapers continued to report rock-throwing incidents in Chico, to further support the fact that plenty of resentment toward Orientals was still in existence at the turn of the twentieth century.

Returning to the West Branch Mill, though, injuries occurred even while it was still in the building stage. Four carpenters were severely injured when the scaffolding they were standing on collapsed, causing them to fall about

Hallam House

Restaurant

ROBT. McEWING,   -   Proprietor

Open at all hours of day
or night. Regular hotel
meals morning, noon and
evening.

Having taken entire management of
this establishment, I intend to con-
duct it as a first-class restaurant and
thus merit a share of the public pat-
ronage.

The table will be supplied with the
best of everything the market affords

ONLY WHITE HELP EMPLOYED

Main Street   -   Chico

Above: This photo, circa 1885, shows
one Chico hotel where injured loggers
were sometimes taken. Called the
Union Hotel, it was located on the
corner of Third and Main Streets.
*Courtesy of CSU, Chico, Meriam Library,
Special Collections. Donated by John Nopel.*

Left: Hallam House Restaurant, part
of the hotel, posted this advertisement
in the *Chico Enterprise*, during the
spring of 1903. (This one was dated
May 30.) Note how the restaurant
advertisement appealed to people who
supported white employment only. If
the news reports were any indication,
it appears most of the injured loggers
were sent to the Hallam House to
recover.

thirty feet. Although none of the injuries was life threatening, it was expected that three of the men would be off work for several weeks.

When we envision a lumberjack, we often think of a brawny man swinging an ax with expertise and driving the sharp edge of the head deep into the wood. However, the slightest bit of fatigue, or maybe a loss of concentration, and the tool might suddenly glance off in an undesirable direction, sometimes toward an exposed body part. Knees were often the unintended targets of misguided ax blades. Wm. Hannigan found this out while he was "swamping" (i.e., limbing) one day. The injury caused his knee to swell up to twice its normal size. Jack Weelis and a young man named Kent managed to slash theirs while "barking" logs. Kent needed eighteen stitches to close up his wound. Joe Malloy had an ax knocked from his grip and driven into his knee while he was felling a tree, opening up a tear several inches long. Other body parts might be in danger from ax blades too, as Matt Moore once discovered when he gashed his foot badly by one while cutting some timber.

Handling heavy logs always posed danger in the lumber industry, and working around the West Branch Mill was no exception. Feet and legs were constantly at risk of getting in the way of a log that decided to unexpectedly shift its position. H. Herrick and C.W. Dorrett suffered serious foot injuries from logs rolling onto them. About a year later, Harry Herrick (presumably the same man as above) managed to break several bones in his leg when a log rolled off one of the chutes.

Ed Lawler, a foreman at one of the camps, caught a leg between two logs while rolling them onto a chute, crushing the limb quite severely. The injury was so bad that some of the protruding pieces of bone had to be removed. Ed had returned to work just two weeks before, after taking a month off due to an earlier leg injury. A highly respected individual, Ed was considered for the superintendent position when Jack Cussick left. The extent of the injury and expected long recovery period prompted the West Branch family from the mill and logging camps to establish a fund of $600 to help pay medical costs. When Superintendent Thatcher visited Ed in Chico and told him about the donations, an emotional Lawler expressed much appreciation for what "the boys" had done.[67]

Upper body injuries from unpredictable logs were also common, and it's a wonder no one was ever killed, or so it appeared. For instance, a log jumped from a chute and rolled onto Andy Morrison, breaking his collarbone and inflicting some bruises. A log rolled over John Norton, and although he did not appear to have any broken bones, it was feared that he suffered some serious internal injuries. A similar accident happened to John McDonald, and he suffered a punctured lung by a broken rib. David Brown was following along behind a log that was being dragged to a chute when it ran over a bush or sapling and suddenly kicked backward, striking him hard in the face. Although David returned to work soon afterward, he began to hemorrhage two weeks later, causing much concern among friends and family. While moving a log toward the saw, "Doc" Bispham, the sawyer at the mill, crushed his arm when it became trapped between the log and a post.

Even horses were in danger. Henry Bruce was hauling a string of logs into a chute with a team of four horses when he happened to look up and see a large log coming down the trough at a high rate of speed. Henry leaped from the saddle horse just in time as the log came racing by. He barely escaped with his life, but the team of company-owned horses was not as fortunate. They were all killed.[68]

Of course, the railroad hauled logs, and men placed themselves in danger of being crushed during the process of unloading, like Will Owen, who broke his leg when a log kicked back and pinned it against a post. He'd been working for the company only three days when the accident happened. That

Horses generally dragged the logs to the chute. The "steam donkeys" would take over from there. *From the Harris Moak collection. Courtesy of Dale Wangberg.*

Man standing on a log chute in the vicinity of the West Branch Mill. *From the Harris Moak collection. Courtesy of Dale Wangberg.*

was not a good way to start. Dan Norr had a spectacular brush with death while unloading a car. The *Chico Record* reported the incident as follows:

> *The accident occurred while a car of logs was being unloaded at the mill pond. The logs were above the average in size. Norr was working about the logs when one of the hooks, attached to a cable and set into the log, became loose. In some manner Norr got between two logs which were about four feet apart and they started rolling down the log-way to the pond. He could not get out and could only run with them. Those who witnessed the accident expected momentarily that the second log would overtake him and crush him to a pulp. Just before the first log rolled over the log-way into the pond, Norr caught onto it and it threw him ahead of it into the water. The second log had gained a greater speed and struck the water beyond him.*[69]

Railroad employees also worked in highly dangerous conditions, but compared to other train activities in the surrounding area, the West Branch Mill railway operations appeared to run relatively smoothly. It appears there were no fatalities at all and only a few reported mishaps during its eight years of operation. It probably helped that it was a small line with limited traffic, and there did not appear to be any long, steep grades to promote runaways. However, it also didn't seem to be plagued with freakish fatalities, like the ones that occurred in Lyonsville and Stirling City, noted earlier.

Despite the lack of fatalities on the West Branch railroad, "Bobbie" Languille was almost killed and suffered a severe back injury when he was riding some cars loaded with logs that derailed and dropped down into Big Chico Creek. It was reported that one of the logs plunging down the bank grazed him close enough to slice the back of his jumper and pants in two.[70] A log once rolled off a car and landed on an unfortunate brakeman named Everett Skelley, breaking his arm and crushing a leg.

Occasionally, a brakeman might unintentionally depart from the train, like John Bleasdale, who fell off and broke his leg. Joe Pittinger suffered a more severe injury when he fell off the rear car. It was reported that Joe dislocated his ankle, suffered a compound fracture and then shattered the protruding bone by striking it against a rock when he landed. C. Wright once thought he was in danger, so he "joined the birds" and wound up breaking his arm. Apparently, Mr. Wright could fly with the birds; he just didn't know how to land like one.

But perhaps the most amazing escape from death or serious injury involved George Kingston and his daughter Miss Ethel, who were riding the "meat car" one morning from one of the upper logging camps back to the mill. When rounding a sharp curve they saw the headlight of a locomotive that was quickly coming toward them. While traveling downhill, the meat car was able to coast and had brakes to slow it down when needed. (It's likely that the "meat car" was actually one of the "slab cars" referred to earlier.) The harrowing incident was reported by the *Chico Record*:

> As Kingston and daughter were spinning down the canyon, the locomotive, coming up from the mill, came in sight, and it was at once certain there would be a collision. Miss Kingston jumped immediately, but her father remained at the brake till the locomotive and car were within about ten feet of each other, when he also jumped.
>
> The engineer of the locomotive was able to slow down his engine slightly before the collision. The car was wrecked, but, being rather light, did no serious damage to the locomotive. A few yards from where the collision occurred is a long trestle, and had the accident happened there, Mr. and Miss Kingston could not have saved themselves.[71]

As to be expected, working around equipment in the woods was dangerous also. Feet and hands sometimes ended up in places they didn't

Early Logging in Northeastern California

One way to keep the cable off the ground was to guide it along steel wheels placed alongside the chute. Note the "chute greaser" sitting on the log and lubricating the chute. *Courtesy of Bancroft Library University of California, Berkeley.*

belong, and often a price was paid. While operating a donkey engine, Charles Woods's foot was crushed when it became caught between a mechanical wheel and a bolt. John Young's toes got caught in some donkey engine gearing, mangling the digits severely. J.C. Blanton was lubricating one of these machines when his hand got caught in the gearing, crushing two fingers. O.C. Woodward was oiling the cable that was used to pull the logs down the slope to the mill when his hand got caught between it and a wheel, mashing two of his fingers.

Upper body and head injuries occurred on occasion, particularly when the equipment shifted or broke. J.H. Will was severely scalded when the donkey engine he was working with tipped over, broke a steam pipe and sprayed hot steam directly at him, burning his arms, upper body and face. John Schary had been running a donkey engine when he was struck by a piece of iron, fracturing his skull. Fletcher "Dutch" Marion was hurt when the draw head from a donkey broke, and part of it struck him in the face and chest. William "Popp" Watts dislocated his shoulder and suffered injuries to his face when a block broke loose and struck him in the upper body.

With all the tension on those cables, sometimes something had to give. Mr. Campbell was in charge of a donkey engine when a cable broke loose and slapped him in the side, fracturing several ribs. On separate occasions, a whipping cable struck Frank Lane and Bert Leach, fracturing their legs.

West Branch Mill donkey engine crew working near Lomo. A note on the back of the photo indicated that this group pulled the logs out of the West Branch of Butte Creek up to the ridge, before chuting them down into Big Chico Creek Canyon. *Courtesy of CSU, Chico, Meriam Library, Special Collections. Donated by Glenn Dietz.*

Donkey engines, chutes, cables and hooks all posed a danger to the West Branch Mill lumbermen. *Courtesy of CSU, Chico, Meriam Library, Special Collections. Donated by Glenn Dietz.*

Early Logging in Northeastern California

Frank was standing twenty feet from the cable, apparently not far enough, when it snapped.

The mill machinery caused its share of accidents too. Naturally, fingers were in particular danger. "Skip" Martin lost his thumb in some machinery. John Barnes was filling in for Enos Collins at the cut-off saw, and within fifteen minutes, he managed to cut off his thumb. Not surprisingly, John relinquished his new position without hesitation. Even the highly experienced Enos Collins lost two fingertips running that dangerous cut-off saw. He immediately went to the company store and casually informed the occupants, "Well, I've lost a couple."[72]

Legs and feet weren't exactly safe either. It was once reported that an unidentified millworker received a deep gash in the leg by a dislodged tooth from a rapidly revolving saw. James Egan lost two toes when his foot slipped from a lever and jammed his foot. Elmer Carlton tore flesh from the bone on his right foot when he caught his foot on a log carriage that unexpectedly started to move.

There were some potentially serious close calls at the mill also. Will Martin's clothes became tangled in some machinery, and if it wasn't for immediate

The boys gathered around the mill's double circular saw. *From the Harris Moak collection. Courtesy of Dale Wangberg.*

67

Another photo of a mill crew posing near the double circular saw. Note how young the two workers on the left appear to be. *Courtesy of CSU, Chico, Meriam Library, Special Collections. Donated by Glenn Dietz.*

action taken by some other employees, he would have suffered more than just the clothing ripped off his upper body and a lacerated arm. Dr. D.W. Wasley, a visiting dentist, was near some rollers that were used for carrying planks from one saw to another when a large slab of wood struck him in the face and knocked him down. Had it not been for one of the employees who pulled him out of greater harm's way, the doctor might have been killed. The tooth doctor, who was vacationing in Butte Meadows at the time, was asked to come to the West Branch Mill to do some dental work for some of the boys. He'd been at the mill only fifteen minutes before he became a patient at the little hospital. The badly bruised dentist then returned to Butte Meadows to recover from his wounds.[73] Some vacation that was.

Other unfortunate injuries happened as well. George McIver suffered for a week from a wound caused by a large splinter in his leg. After erysipelas set in, he finally sought medical attention to alleviate the pain. John Apperson lost an eye when a piece of steel flew off a wedge he was driving into a log with a sledgehammer. As luck would have it, John had just recently returned to work after breaking both ankles in a fall. A few years before the log rolled over him, John Norton was walking down a chute with a heavy cross-cut saw when he slipped and fell. Upon hitting the ground, the sharp teeth from the saw cut his arm to the bone.

Company employees often walked the flume, and someone was bound to take a fall. This is precisely what happened to A. Baker one day while working the flume near the China Switch station. Mr. Baker stepped on a weak board that broke under his weight and fell about eighteen feet, breaking his leg and spraining his back. His companion, Samuel Eads, had to carry the wounded man to the station. D.I. Knorr (probably the same man who was almost crushed on the log rollway) was lucky to still be alive after walking the flume on a hunting trip with James Weldin one Sunday morning. Mr. Knorr slipped on a slick footboard, fell about twenty feet and landed headfirst on a boulder below, suffering a gash across his scalp that went from ear to ear and a fracture of the skull that was about an inch long.[74] Frank Popplewell was working on the flume near the Palace station one day and fell twenty-five feet after an overhanging limb snagged a can he was carrying and threw him off balance. Although he didn't break any bones, the fall made it too difficult for the old guy to walk, so

This interesting piece of architectural work, called the "Arch," was located in a very rugged and remote section of Big Chico Creek Canyon, about four and a half miles downstream from the West Branch Mill. *Courtesy of CSU, Chico, Meriam Library, Special Collections. Donated by John Nopel.*

Flume trestle crossing over Big Chico Creek, in the canyon below Ten-Mile House. *Courtesy of CSU, Chico, Meriam Library, Special Collections. Donated by Alzora Snyder.*

he laid on the ground for about five hours before he was found by some other crewmembers. Not surprisingly, all three of these injured men were flumed to Chico to get treatment for their injuries.

However, not all employee flume mishaps resulted in serious injuries. One ended up with a happy ending, although A.J. Weber's fall from the flume created quite a stir in town. It seems that when Mr. Weber fell from the waterway somewhere in the hills, his hat came off and dropped onto the moving water, managing to make it all the way to Chico. The fall had bruised one of Weber's feet, so he couldn't catch up to the floating headpiece. When the hat was discovered in town, Weber's worried friends rounded up a search team, which eventually found the man sleeping comfortably at his home in town. The object of the search wondered what all the fuss was about. He just came to Chico to recover the hat and was surprised to be woken up at such a late hour.

Early Logging in Northeastern California

Frank Thatcher (before he was superintendent) and Wm. Fitzpatrick had an amazing escape from a serious, if not potentially deadly, flume accident one day. A reporter for the *Chico Weekly Chronicle-Record* described the event as follows:

> *They had finished their work at the Cussick mill and decided to come to Chico in the flume. They made the start all right, but when in the canyon near the Forest Ranch, they were horrified to see a break in the flume a short distance ahead.*
>
> *The water was running rapidly and to jump from the flume means almost certain death, for the distance was about sixty feet to the ground. Before they had time to realize their danger the boat shot over the break in the flume and landed them safely on the other side of the gap. Had not the water been running rapidly they would have been dashed through the break to the ground.*
>
> *After climbing down the supports to the ground, the men returned to the mill and reported the break. They came to Chico later by stage.*[75]

Frank Thatcher, who appeared to have as many lives as a cat, proved that you don't need to necessarily fall from a flume to get hurt. One day, he was crossing a log that spanned a small ravine, fell about twelve feet and landed on his back on another log below. As to be expected, people fell off railroad trestles also. One day, Willie Skipworth and a companion dropped from one about seventeen feet to the ground below. Willie was pretty bruised, but the other man was amazingly unhurt. Allen Brown managed to break his arm when he fell twenty-five feet from a trestle at the mill.

As if contending with perilous heights, hazardous equipment and heavy, unpredictable logs were not enough, the boys had to deal with dangerous creatures residing in the woods also. For instance, it was not long after the mill first opened that it was reported that men in the canyon had to be on constant watch for rattlesnakes, which were residing in just about any place a logger might be working, and that there was a constant threat of being bitten by one of these most feared reptiles. Barney Cussick was known to make sure the camps were well supplied with whiskey, in case any of the loggers should fall victim to a viper's poisonous fangs.[76] Although many people today would probably not condone this longtime folk remedy, we can assume good ol' Barney meant well anyway.

However, Sierra Lumber Company employees had even bigger and potentially deadlier wild beasts to worry about. A local newspaper recounted an unusual event that surprised W.C. Herrick, George Coen and Philip

Coen, who were camped in Web Canyon (now referred to as Webb Hollow) to get out shakes for the company's new logging camp there. Apparently, the three men and their two dogs, one of which was just a pup, were sitting around the campfire one evening when suddenly the dogs started barking at something lurking in the shadows of the darkness. Before long, a large California mountain lion appeared within thirty feet of the campfire, grabbed the little yelping pup with its jaws and ran off into the night. The startled men immediately attempted to follow the big cat in order to save the unfortunate little dog but were only able to go a short ways before the blackness of the night forced them to turn back. Attempts to track down the lion the following day were unsuccessful.[77]

But that was not the only scary incident involving a large feline. The *Chico Daily Record* described one that struck even closer to home. It was reported by the newspaper that after a hard day's work, many of the "jackies" would often walk the trails from camp to camp, in pursuit of nightly entertainment. However, there was a short period when these after-dark activities around the West Branch Mill slowed down considerably. Now, it wasn't because these lumbermen had suddenly found "moral rejuvenation." That was not the case at all. It was due to the fact that some had become fearful that a mountain lion was stalking them from the opposite side of the creek. At first, the stories of these tough woodsmen fearing that they looked like cat food to some hungry carnivore seemed unbelievable, despite the apparent sincerity of the men who made the claims, some of whom even heard "blood-curdling yells" that were enough to "fairly paralyze them." It was speculated by the local people at the time that the yells were most likely coming from a newcomer to the camps who was just practicing some roots for inter-camp baseball games. However, a daylight investigation revealed that there was indeed a large lion roaming about and that his trail was becoming increasingly closer to that of the men.[78]

As anyone knows, even domestic animals can cause injury, and horses are no exception. Sim Moak, the Chico factory employee referred to earlier, would certainly attest to that. Horse-inflicted injuries struck the Sierra Lumber foothill operations as well. Charles Enquest required crutches to get around, after a horse that was being used to load logs on a truck fell and rolled over him. Charles Kruger, who was driving a team of ten horses from Chico to the mill at West Branch, was somehow struck in the face by one of his horses and was found lying unconscious on the Humboldt Road by a couple of men passing by. A shoe cork (a rural colloquialism for "calk"—a projection from a horseshoe designed to give the animal added traction) had been driven through Charles's lower lip, tilting three teeth and fracturing his jawbone. Like Sim, the unfortunate team driver never knew what hit him.

Early Logging in Northeastern California

A spectacular accident occurred at about 5:30 one morning on the grade from the West Branch stage stop on the ridge down to the mill in the canyon. (It was reported that this road was so steep in places that freighters would often tie a log to the back of their wagons to use as a brake.) A stage was returning with ten passengers, men and women, from a dance at Lomo. When it reached a curve called Beany Turn, one of the horses began to kick. The driver, James Carter, was doing all he could to keep the stage on the road when one of the passengers inexplicably tried to assist by taking hold of the lines. This only made matters worse. The out-of-control stage went over the edge of the road and tumbled into a steep ravine, eventually coming up against a tree. Luckily, the thick brush in the ravine was able to soften the stage's descent down the slope, so most of the passengers received cuts and bruises, but none was badly hurt. However, the stage driver was seriously injured, the stage was a wreck and a horse was killed.[79]

Despite some of the serious accidents reported around the West Branch Mill, this author found no evidence that anyone ultimately died from these injuries. This is quite amazing considering all the fatalities that occurred at nearby lumbering operations during this same time period, including at least one reported death that occurred at the Chico box factory, when a sixteen-year-old-boy named Charles Sutton fell onto a cut-off saw in 1902.

Before the final logging season ended, though, the West Branch family had to suffer through an ordeal that began with a tragic, but accidental, death of one of their very own. However, it was not occupationally related. Harry Hoyt, an employee of Sierra Lumber for several years, left for a solo hunting trip one Sunday morning but failed to return home by that evening. Fearing that the young man may have been injured or even gotten lost, Superintendent Frank Thatcher personally led a search party that night and was able to follow Harry's trail to a point about five miles above the mill before the search was called off. The next morning, the mill was closed down, and all available men were sent out to assist in the search. By late afternoon, Harry's body was discovered—the victim of a fatal gunshot wound. To make matters worse, the body could not be removed from its location until the coroner gave permission to do so. As luck would have it, the coroner from Butte County was the first to be called on to investigate the affair, but it was soon realized that the incident was out of his jurisdiction, since it actually occurred in Tehama County. It wasn't until Wednesday morning that the Tehama County coroner finally arrived, and the remains were taken away by the undertaker.[80]

The inquest was held at the West Branch schoolhouse that same day and lasted until midnight. Two young men, Benjamin Crabbe and James D.

Finnicum, were known to be hunting in the same vicinity at the time and were under suspicion during the entire time of the questioning. Although the evidence strongly pointed to either one or the other firing the lethal bullet, the nervous young men stuck to the story that they knew nothing about the accident. Finally, the coroner decided it was useless to go any further, so the jury came to a verdict and concluded that Harry was apparently shot accidentally by an unknown person with a high-velocity rifle, presumably because he was mistaken for a deer. Harry was a likable guy and had no enemies, so there was no reason for anyone to purposely kill him.

Before he left, however, the coroner advised the friends of Crabbe and Finnicum to convince the young men to tell the truth. A day later, they could no longer hold back and gave a full confession to Superintendent Thatcher. The two hunters related that they saw something move in the brush that looked like a brown bear, and Crabbe hastily fired away. When they realized that Hoyt had been killed and that nothing could be done for him, the frightened men left the scene of the crime, hoping that the truth would forever remain a mystery. Nonetheless, the guilt must have been tremendous, for not only did Crabbe kill a friend and former schoolmate, but the two just left the body lying there, knowing it would soon be food for animals.[81]

Then, of course, there was fear of the consequences, and rightfully so. Not only did the two young men face possible jail time, but when word got out about the confession, there were some fairly angry people about who had spent quite a bit of energy and time searching for Harry, while Ben and J.D., search party members themselves, never led anyone to where they knew the body lay. When the guilty parties left the West Branch for Chico the following day, it was heard that they had to avoid an angry brother-in-law of the victim, Al Harris, who had threatened to kill them if he saw them on the stage. (It was found out later that Harris had been lying in wait at the Ten-Mile House, armed with a rifle.) So when the two distressed men reached the ridge, they got off the stage at Berdan's and walked cross-country to Stirling City, where they boarded the afternoon train to the valley from there. Ironically, Harris was Crabbe's companion during the search. Once in Chico, Crabbe and Finnicum were met by the constable and escorted to the city jail, so that they could eventually be transported to the Red Bluff jail when the Tehama County sheriff arrived.[82]

The tragedy had quite an impact on the entire area, for the young men were in good standing with the community and came from respectable families. Ben Crabbe, twenty years old and a student at Chico Normal (now called California State University, Chico), was known as a hardworking and good young man. At the time of the accident, he was working at the West

Branch Mill to earn money for his studies. His family was well known in the mining sections of the area. J.D. Finnicum, a nephew of an established veterinarian in Chico, had a good reputation as well. The community must have been torn, for admittedly the young men were guilty of committing a huge hunting mistake with dreadful consequences, but it appears most people recognized that it was an accident, with no maliciousness involved. Many felt that perhaps the biggest crime was holding back the truth, when the two men could have cleared things up immediately.

In fact, that's just what the Tehama charges were—perjury at the West Branch inquest. The Tehama County district attorney, however, was also looking to convict them of murder. From the onset, neither charge appeared able to stick. The former was weak because, as it turned out, the inquest was conveniently held at the schoolhouse in Butte County, not Tehama, where the killing occurred—a technicality, but a solid one. As far as the latter charge was concerned, just about everyone believed that the shooting was nothing more than an accident, so it didn't seem reasonable to go through the expense of a lengthy trial where the chances of a conviction were small. It was widely felt that, although the two young men should have gone through the agony of being arrested for their terrible lapse in judgment, going to prison would serve no justice. Nonetheless, when the perjury charge was dismissed, Crabbe and Finnicum were charged with manslaughter instead. Eventually, that charge was also dropped, and the two men were set free.[83]

The whole ordeal lasted a little over two weeks and was extensively covered by the local press. Although the two young men certainly angered many people for various reasons, the accidental killing itself was generally accepted as being an avoidable, but understandable, incident. Even today, how many times have we read or heard about a similar event? It happens.

CHAPTER 5
THE COMPANY DOCTOR

With all the mishaps that occur around a major logging operation, it's no wonder that Sierra Lumber would need the services of a full-time doctor at its West Branch Mill. In February 1901, a young physician answered the call and arrived at the site to begin a medical practice that helped protect the loggers and their families for the duration of the mill operations. His name was Dr. Newton T. Enloe.

Dr. Enloe was a native of Missouri. According to different sources, he graduated in 1895 from either Missouri Medical College or Washington University Medical School, both located in St. Louis. He subsequently practiced medicine in Jefferson City. It was here that he married his first wife, formerly Miss Winnie Herrick. A deteriorating lung condition compelled Dr. Enloe to move westward to a healthier climate. Joining him were one of his sisters and his two-year-old son, Newton Jr.[84]

While in Chico, Dr. Enloe was informed that the West Branch Mill workers and their families desired a doctor who could live on the premises. He soon went to the mill site and became the resident physician, and it is believed he was the first person to fill this kind of role in northern California's pine industry. The doctor offered the lumbermen and their families a comprehensive medical care plan for a mere one dollar a month, births and hospitalization included, thought to be the first pre-paid medical plan in California. Thanks to this novel idea, it's been said that the good doctor was almost disqualified for membership in the California Medical Association.

The talented young physician was not only good with medicine, but he also knew how to cut with a saw and swing a hammer. With scrap lumber from the mill, Dr. Enloe constructed a rudimentary little hospital on the mill site, with a five-bed capacity. It's been said that he often created his own equipment and instruments with the help of a blacksmith, and he had to perform surgery on a wooden table. It was reported that once the innovative doctor used a twenty-penny nail to repair the broken leg of one of his loggers, a technique he picked up back east. The confident physician didn't hesitate to demonstrate how skillful he was either. Other surgeons who worked with him said that sometimes he would light up a cigar before surgery, lay it down for the operation and finish off the smoke afterward, without ever having to relight the cigar.

Dr. Newton T. Enloe, from Mansfield's 1918 book *History of Butte County.*

The little hospital that Dr. Enloe built at the mill site. *Courtesy of CSU, Chico, Meriam Library, Special Collections.*

During the second year as the mill's resident physician, he opened an office in Chico and hurried back up to the mill whenever his services were called for. It is not clear exactly when the doctor decided to spend a major portion of his time in the valley, but his first professional card, printed in local papers, indicates it could have been as early as spring 1902, when he advertised that he had an office located in the newly built Morehead Building, on the corner of Fourth and Broadway Streets, in Chico. Not long after opening, he purchased an X-ray machine for this office. The doctor continued to advertise his services in the 1903 and 1904 Chico newspapers. In early 1904, he shared several office rooms in the Morehead Building with Dr. D.H. Moulton. However, by April of that year, Dr. Moulton was advertising by himself, and Dr. Enloe was nowhere to be seen in the newspaper professional card listings—and it stayed that way for the rest of the time the West Branch Mill was in operation. Therefore, it's probably safe to assume that from 1902 through early 1904, his primary place of residence was in the valley, but he may have also kept a place near the mill during that time, since he was still working for Sierra Lumber. However, it appears after that he chose to return to the foothills and make West Branch his primary place of residence for the rest of the time the mill was in operation, possibly because he realized that all the time he was spending in the valley was taking away from a commitment he'd made to the lumbermen and their families, not to mention others living in the higher elevations who were in need of his services. Indeed, in 1905, the *Chico Daily Enterprise* wrote: "The sick and wounded around the mill and the logging camps keep Dr. Enloe very

N. T. Enloe, M. D.
D. H. Moulton, M. D.

ENLOE & MOULTON.

Physicians and Surgeons, Chico, Cal. Office Rooms: 1, 2, 3 and 4, Morehead Building. Office Hours: 8 to 10 a. m.; 12 to 2 and 7 to 8 p. m. Phone Red 911.

In early 1904, before he returned to West Branch, Dr. Enloe shared an office with Dr. Moulton. This professional card was advertised in the March 19 edition of the *Chico Daily Record*.

Early Logging in Northeastern California

The Morehead Building, on the corner of Fourth and Broadway Streets, in Chico. It was built in 1901. Dr. Enloe had an office located inside during the years 1902–04. *Courtesy of CSU, Chico, Meriam Library, Special Collections. Donated by John Nopel.*

busy nowadays."[85] Further evidence that he stayed with the lumbermen to the very end is provided by the 1906 Butte County register of marriages, which listed West Branch as his place of residence. A newspaper reported that he was also planning to spend the winter of '06–'07 at Soda Springs (more on that story later), located near Butte Meadows, with his new bride, the former Isabelle Mansfield.

The doctor realized that some of his logging patients needed greater care than the West Branch hospital could provide. So reports suggested he transported some of his patients to either his Chico office, the Hallam House or the Sisters' Hospital, in Chico. The ones who were severely injured were brought to San Francisco.

Accounts of his assistance to the lumbermen and their families were often documented in the newspapers. For instance, during the first year he stayed at the mill, it was reported that he treated John Norton, who was seriously injured from being pinned under a log; he amputated four of John Young's mangled toes that were caught in some gearing, although he did all he could to save the biggest one; he stitched up Dutch Marion's face after the worker's encounter with a broken draw head; he cared for Joe Pittinger's severe leg injury, which resulted from a fall from a train; and he prepared Everett Skelley for the flume ride from the mill to Chico after a log rolled on the brakeman. During the second and third years, when he stayed mostly in Chico, it was reported that he doctored John Bleasdale at his Morehead office after the West Branch railroad worker fell off a train and broke his leg; he treated John McDonald's broken rib and punctured lung at the Hallam House; and he cared for Elmer Carlton, whose foot was crushed at the mill.

It was Dr. Enloe who rushed from the valley in 1903 to help the stunned riders when the stage went out of control down the steep canyon road to the mill. Recall that the only person badly injured in the incident was the stage driver, James Carter. The doctor elected to let Carter recover at West Branch rather than transport him to Chico. After returning to West Branch from Chico, about a week later, to place the driver's broken leg in a cast, the *Chico Daily Record* quoted Dr. Enloe as saying, "There is something peculiar about the climate at West Branch. It seems to be constantly in favor of the patient. Wounds of any kind apparently heal much quicker and patients seem to be able to stand more. For that reason, I had great hopes for Carter's recovery."[86]

After the doctor returned to live near the mill in 1904, he hurriedly left a meeting of the Butte County Medical Association in Chico, where he was to present a paper, to rush back and attend to Mr. Campbell as soon as possible after the logger was struck by the donkey engine cable; he personally delivered Bobby Languille to Chico on a flume boat after his unfortunate ride with the derailed log cars into the creek; he also accompanied C. Wright, the brakeman who leaped from a moving log car, although it is unclear which mode of transportation to the valley was used; and he came to the assistance of Charles Weber's badly burned child near Forest Ranch, who unfortunately did not survive.

Maybe the most publicized event was in 1901 when Dr. Enloe attended to the severely injured Ed Lawler, who crushed his leg between two heavy logs. The doctor advised that Ed be immediately transported to Chico by flume in order to give his mangled leg the best chance to be saved. He made sure that Ed, who must have been in great agony, was as comfortable as possible for the trip. After Dr. Enloe prepared the injured logger the best he could, two friends accompanied the wounded man on the flume boat down to the valley. Ed did not stay long in Chico, as he was soon transferred to San Francisco in order to get the best care possible. Along with Ed's brother, Barney Cussick accompanied the severely injured man to the big city. (It just goes to show that good ol' Barney still cared a lot about his logger friends, six years after he retired from the business.) Although it was initially feared Ed might lose his leg, or even his life, when he was finally allowed to go

Early Logging in Northeastern California

This is a photo of Dr. Enloe riding a flume boat from the West Branch Mill to Chico, with his son, Newt Jr., sitting on his lap. It's generally believed that the woman was Dr. Enloe's sister, Emma, and the man was Dan Knorr. Emma and Dan were married at some time. *Courtesy of CSU, Chico, Meriam Library, Special Collections. Donated by John Nopel.*

home over a half year later, the news indicated that the popular logger had a good chance of complete recovery. Nonetheless, Ed was on crutches for quite some time afterward, and he was still using them when he returned to work for the company.[87]

As with Ed Lawler, a patient might not know for quite some time whether a limb could be saved. Unfortunately for Joseph Pettinger, it was years before he knew. Due to the severe ankle injury he had suffered long before, the bone in his foot eventually became too diseased to allow it to remain. In order to save his life, Dr. Enloe was finally forced to amputate.

Of course, as a dedicated lifesaver, the doctor came to the aid of more people in the foothills and mountains than just West Branch Mill employees and their families. He traveled all around the countryside to help those in need. While he was still working in Chico, he went as far as Chico Meadows on at least five occasions to care for the gravely ill Marcus Washburn.

Unfortunately, the aged gentleman died while arrangements were being made to transfer him to the Sierra Lumber Company hospital at West Branch. When he was back living near the mill, Dr. Enloe came to the aid of a stranger to these parts, a man named Theophilas Contu. Mr. Contu was apparently sleeping in a barn loft at Berdan's stage stop when he fell through a hole used as a hay chute down to the lower level. Dr. Enloe accompanied the unconscious man to Chico for treatment, but about two weeks later, the comatose man could not hang on any longer. It wasn't always exactly smooth sailing for the physician either. One time he was accompanying a sick John Hollenbeck down from the hills in a buggy, when the kingbolt on the rig broke. The horses did not hesitate to leave the two riders behind, forcing Dr. Enloe and his patient to hoof it on their own. Things just weren't going well for John around that time. This event happened less than a year after he was robbed and roughed up some at the Ten-Mile House, and at that time, the old guy was reported to have health issues.

There were surely many mountain exploits that were not reported in the local press. From what we do know, most people would probably agree that the early California history of Dr. Newton T. Enloe gives "commuting to work" an entirely different meaning.

It wasn't particularly safe being a physician around the mill either. Dr. Enloe had a narrow escape from serious injury one day, when a large piece of bark fell from a big Douglas fir tree, struck him in the shoulder and knocked him to the ground. Fortunately, he only sustained some painful bruises. This time, however, it was the doctor who had to be transported to Chico for treatment. He was placed under the care of his former partner, Dr. Moulton.[88]

But perhaps the most frightening event for the doctor occurred on a Monday morning, June 17, 1901, just a few months after he first arrived at the West Branch Mill to assume his duties. On that day, a man carrying a rifle relieved the doctor of some of his hard-earned capital.

Immediately after the scary encounter, Dr. Enloe went to Chico and related his ordeal to District Attorney Sproul and the media, including some background information that led up to the incident. Apparently, over the previous few weeks the doctor had been receiving numerous requests from Mrs. Card, the wife of lumberjack Andrew Card, to come to their residence at one of the logging camps up the canyon. The doctor said the visits proved to be totally unnecessary, so he informed Mrs. Card on Sunday, June 16, that he would not come again unless he was sure that her family needed medical attention. Furthermore, the doctor said that he had informed Mrs. Card earlier that he would not treat her, in particular, unless her husband or a lady friend was present, thereby allowing him to follow his professional principles. By that time, he was becoming suspicious that she had some hidden agenda in mind.

Dr. Enloe related that on the following morning, he saw Andrew Card near his cabin carrying a rifle, so he said to him, "Hello, Card; out hunting this morning?" The reply was, "Yes, and you are my game." Dr. Enloe said that, at first, he thought it was some kind of joke, but soon it became evident to him that the man meant business. Dr. Enloe reported that Card then complained that the resident physician was making easy money, while he had to work hard for a living, so it was time to "divide up." Card subsequently accused the doctor of assaulting his wife and said that she and his brother would back up his claim. Dr. Enloe said he tried to reason with the man, but to no avail. Then Card allegedly pointed the gun at him and threatened to blow his brains out if the doctor didn't give him some cash. So the scared physician handed over to the menacing logger sixty dollars in gold coin. But this was not all of it. In a bizarre twist, the doctor said that Card demanded that the physician also sign over half his future earnings until November 1, under the pretense of purchasing a ranch from the lumberman. Card left his rifle at the cabin, and the two went to the company office, where Dr. Enloe handed over the order. It was reported that before he left for home, Card informed the doctor that when the order expired, he just might demand more.[89]

As soon as Card was out of sight, Dr. Enloe went to the company bookkeeper, Steve Magee, and told him what had happened and how he was forced to write out the phony order that gave away half his future earnings to Card. Magee recommended the doctor head to Chico to file an official complaint to the authorities, which the physician promptly did, by flume boat.[90]

On Tuesday, the eighteenth, Andrew Card was arrested and placed in jail on a robbery charge and $1,000 bail, which he was unable to post. While there, the prisoner was interviewed and claimed that he received $20 in gold from the physician, the order for half of Dr. Enloe's future income until November and a promise for another $80 in cash. Card said he had originally gone to the resident physician's cabin to run him out of West Branch for ruining his relationship with his wife but that the doctor offered to square things up with money to keep him quiet. Card said he was justified in confronting the doctor because, after his suspicions were aroused from the frequent visits to his residence, he decided to wait in the bushes Sunday morning to see if he could catch the doctor doing something improper. Card told the reporter that after observing his wife lock up the children in one tent and then seeing her and the doctor enter the parlor tent, he snuck up closer and looked through a peephole to see his wife and the doctor in an act of intimacy. He then retreated to the bushes rather than make a scene at the time. Card said he threatened to leave his wife that evening, but the tears from her and the children convinced him to stay, so running the doctor out of the country was going to be his payback.[91]

From the beginning, it was evident that the local media sympathized with Dr. Enloe. One paper indicated that, regardless of what may have really happened at the tent, it did not give Card the right to hold up the physician for all he had, plus his future earnings. Another wondered, if Card really saw what he claimed, why it took him so long to act on it and questioned how he was willing to place a price on the honor of his wife.

The following day, it was Mrs. Card's turn to describe her version of the story. When she heard that her husband said she would support his accusations against the doctor, she emphatically denied being any part of such a plan and stated that Andrew was a liar. She agreed that the doctor was summoned to the Card residence on that Sunday but said it was to care for her sick baby. The lumberman's wife denied locking up her children or that she was guilty of anything improper. She explained that her husband was previously showing signs of disliking Dr. Enloe and demanded she not see him anymore, to which she did not comply. She claimed that on Sunday evening, Andrew Card accused her of infidelity and told her he would kill himself if she did not confess and implicate the doctor. Mrs. Card said she didn't fall for the bluff. The newspaper reported that soon after Andrew's arrest she moved out to live with her parents, who resided in the town of Paradise.[92]

As Andrew Card previously indicated, his brother Gus was there to support him. Unfortunately for Andrew, though, Gus didn't turn out to be as reliable as hoped for. It seems that shortly after arriving in town the day after Andrew's arrest, Gus's affection for beer took precedence, and it was not long before he landed in jail for being drunk and disorderly. A local paper appeared to find the whole affair quite humorous, finishing the article with the statement: "This is certainly a case of a pair."[93]

When it was time for a preliminary examination on June 26 to determine if the lumberman should be held for trial before the Superior Court, Andrew Card wasn't ready for it. He didn't have an attorney or witnesses, so the examination was clearly one-sided, in favor of the physician. Mrs. Ida McGulgan testified that Dr. Enloe was at her residence that Sunday at the time Card claimed he was peeping through the hole in the tent. Frank Thatcher identified the order that Enloe filled out. Ben and George Norton testified that they were working with Card in the woods the entire day. Mrs. Card's brother, Antone Parker, testified that Andrew told him about catching his wife and the doctor in the act earlier that day and asked for his brother-in-law's advice. Parker said he told Card he had never been in such a situation but most likely would have acted on it immediately. Mrs. Card's father, James Parker, testified that he loaned Card a rifle, probably the one that was used in the alleged holdup. Mrs. Card testified that Dr. Enloe was there that day but only for a few minutes. When Andrew Card asked his wife if he had ever forbidden her to call on the doctor, she admitted that he had. She also said that at one time Andrew had threatened to take his name off the hospital list if the doctor continued to make visits. After the testimony was complete, Judge Collins made the order to hold the defendant over for trial.[94]

On July 22, Superior Court Judge Gray ordered another preliminary hearing be held on account of Card's lack of representation the first time around.[95] The media reported that the case was getting to be a nuisance for Sierra Lumber because many of the workers were going to be pulled from their jobs to testify during a busy time of year, in a case about which they knew nothing of importance.[96]

It certainly wasn't easy on Harry O'Neil, who on the night before the second preliminary was riding down the flume with Dr. Enloe in order to appear as a witness at the hearing. The news reported that a sleepy O'Neil fell into the water. The doctor managed to stop the boat and get Harry back on board, only to have the same thing repeat itself farther downstream at China Switch. This time, however, the doctor could not stop the watercraft. The soaking wet trial witness managed to get another boat, but needless to say, he was a bit worse for the wear when he finally arrived in Chico, an hour after Dr. Enloe.

When the second hearing, which took place on July 31, was all said and done, the result was the same—Andrew Card was once more held to be tried in Superior Court. However, it was not before some interesting testimony was given, although much of it was just a repeat of the first hearing. Constable Goe and Defense Attorney Duncan tangled some because the police officer couldn't keep from expressing his own opinion. Mrs. Card declined to testify. Steve Magee, the company bookkeeper, testified that Card was with Dr. Enloe when the physician gave the order. Charles Marion, the locomotive engineer for the logging train, said he delivered notes from Mrs. Card to the doctor but couldn't remember dates or any definite information.

Harry O'Neil, the clerk in the company store, which was probably located close to the office, appeared to take center stage for the day. (Recall that this was the man who had some difficulty staying on board the flume boat on the way to the hearing.) Harry claimed to know nothing about the case, except that when the order to divide the doctor's earnings was placed on Superintendent Thatcher's desk, he read it. When asked by Card's attorney if that was all he knew about the case, the reluctant witness sarcastically replied, "If I remember any more, you can search me." When shown the order, the stubborn clerk denied ever seeing the writing before. After he was reminded that was the order he claimed to have read earlier, Harry took a longer look, before saying, "Well, it looks a hell of a lot different to me." After his testimony was complete, O'Neil shook hands with Andrew Card and said he hoped that the defendant would be given a fair shake.[97]

When the Superior Court trial finally got underway on October 7, it was quite the media sensation and was covered extensively in at least four different local papers. Not long after the trial began, the judge feared that many of the witnesses might not be able to resist the temptations of the many drinking establishments that the county seat had to offer and would make unreliable witnesses as a result. So his honor informed them before they were allowed to leave the courtroom that they could roam the courtyard at will but not visit any of the nearby saloons. If one should show up unfit to testify, he would, as a *Chico Daily Record* reporter so eloquently put it, "rest in the refrigerator until he had fully recovered." The threat must have had some impact—everyone showed up sober.[98]

After jury selection, Dr. Enloe was the first to go on the stand and related much of the same testimony as before. Dr. Enloe testified he gave the order to Frank Thatcher before it was given to Steve Magee. When Attorney Duncan asked the doctor why he didn't refuse to be held up when he was in the presence of others, the doctor replied that he didn't know any of the men very well and wanted to avoid any potential shooting. So he waited until Card left the scene. The Norton brothers again declared that Card, who was working near them all day in the woods, was never away long enough to be able to go to his residence and back without being missed. H.C. Fischer's testimony indicated that the time required to make the trip was considerably less than what the Norton brothers claimed it would take in their testimony. Mr. Miller—who, after hearing what the Norton brothers said in the preliminary trial, made the walk and timed himself—also indicated at this trial that the Norton brothers overestimated the time to make the trip. A number of witnesses were called upon to attest to Card's good character, including Steve Magee and the mayor of Chico, O.L. Clark. Andrew Card testified that, after stewing over it for some time, he finally came to the point of wanting to kill Dr. Enloe, so he went to the physician's cabin on that Monday morning to do just that, but he said the doctor persuaded him to accept a monetary settlement instead. Despite having the rifle with him, Andrew Card denied ever threatening the physician or demanding money, claiming that the doctor voluntarily offered him compensation to square things up.[99]

Early Logging in Northeastern California

On the afternoon of the third day of testimony (four days after jury selection began), the trial was handed over to the jury. A day later, six jurors voted for conviction and an equal number for acquittal. They were sent home, and almost a week later, it became official—the case was dismissed, and Andrew Card was set free.[100]

Not long after the trial ended, Della Card filed for divorce from her husband. Again, Andrew Card's indifference was revealed, as he failed to show up for the proceedings. The *Chico Enterprise*, which was still obviously not in favor of Andrew Card, emphasized that Mrs. Card wanted to separate from the man who was willing to sell her good name for money.[101] On December 30, it became official. The two Chico newspapers reported that she was granted a divorce "on the grounds of extreme cruelty."[102]

The biggest question concerning the doctor seemed to be why he hadn't immediately told others that he was being robbed when he was in the presence of more than just Andrew Card. His answer was that he was relatively new around there, so he wasn't sure he could trust the people and didn't know whether or not Card might be concealing a pistol.

On the other hand, people wondered why Andrew Card didn't do something right away after supposedly catching his wife and the doctor in the act. Why did he wait so long to take action?

Andrew Card, who had been working at the West Branch Mill for about four years and in Tehama County sometime before that, had a good number of supporters and friends from both areas. He didn't appear to have a history of such outrageous behavior, or at least there was none mentioned by the news at the time of the trial. There seems to be little else known about Andrew Card today.

Dr. Enloe was a newcomer who did not yet have a chance to gain the confidence of the entire West Branch family, putting him at a disadvantage with the well-established logger. However, as the West Branch people got to know the doctor much better over time, he was warmly accepted. Therefore, it would seem unlikely that the loggers would have trusted him with their families afterward if they felt he was capable of such misconduct.

Furthermore, history has shown that throughout his career, Dr. Enloe was a dedicated MD and appeared to be the consummate professional. He worked hard and sacrificed much of his time to become a highly regarded physician and is still an iconic figure in northern California today. It would be very out of character for him to have taken such a huge risk so soon after arriving, a gamble that would have carried the potential to forever tarnish his medical reputation.

The highly esteemed historian W.H. Hutchinson believed the doctor may have been the victim of a failed attempt to employ a version of an extortion scheme that is referred to as the "Badger Game,"[103] one that is set up to look like the husband walks in on his spouse and the unsuspecting man while they are in a situation that could be construed as shameful behavior. This was a con that was often directed at doctors since, by profession, they were particularly vulnerable. In 1930, the problem was even publicized in *Time* magazine.[104]

Keep in mind, however, that the trial was not about whether or not the doctor had an affair with Mrs. Card. It was about whether or not he was held up at gunpoint by Andrew Card. Nonetheless, the testimony appeared to center on the motive for the exchange of money and the truthfulness of the participants. Ultimately, the jury could not decide on a verdict. Six of them believed that there was enough evidence to show beyond a reasonable doubt that Andrew Card had robbed the doctor. The other six either believed Andrew Card's version of the events or simply didn't think the arguments were strong enough to show beyond a reasonable doubt that Andrew Card took the money from Dr. Enloe by force.

We may never know for sure the whole truth about what did or did not take place that fateful Sunday and following Monday. Only three people really did, and they are long gone. Who knows? It may have been just a huge misunderstanding.

The building that housed the Paradise Sanitarium is still located on the Skyway, in Paradise. The hospital was constructed around 1921. It now contains the main office and some residential apartments in the Evergreen Mobile Home Park. *Photo taken by the author.*

Early Logging in Northeastern California

Andrew Card allegedly claimed the doctor was making "easy money." You couldn't convince this author of that, after everything that Dr. Enloe went through in 1901. Despite his rough initiation to California medicine, it didn't disrupt the doctor's drive at all. He continued on and gained the confidence of the people under his care. After his arrival in 1901, he remained the company physician for the rest of the time the canyon mill was in operation. All indications were that Dr. Enloe was well trusted and highly respected by the West Branch family.

After the Sierra Lumber operations in Big Chico Creek closed down for good, the doctor was forced to move on. We can say with confidence that "the rest is history." The list of Dr. Enloe's many accomplishments is far too long to cover in this writing, and much of it has been written about already. He may be most recognized, however, for at one time constructing a hospital in Paradise, California, for treating tuberculosis patients; developing the first nursing school between Sacramento, California, and Portland, Oregon; and for the hospital that now bears his name, located on Chico's Esplanade.

It's truly impressive how Dr. Enloe's California enterprises blossomed over the years, starting from the crude little hospital in the woods constructed with scrap material to the now multifaceted Enloe Medical Center, the second-largest nongovernment employer in Butte County (in 2011), whose facilities and services benefit a large portion of the population throughout northern California.

CHAPTER 6
CELEBRATIONS AND OTHER GOOD TIMES

Unlike lumber operations in the Pacific Northwest, the West Branch Mill had few transient workers. A good portion of the employees had families that stayed at the mill site throughout the winter, so many of the leisure activities were geared to entertain women and children, too.

Lumbermen worked hard, and they played hard. The Sierra Lumber boys and their families found plenty of reason to celebrate holidays and enjoy other events, with a number of these attracting the local press. The people living and working around the mill appeared to have a predilection for drinking and dancing. Dining halls in logging camps were often the venue for parties, since they were very spacious, especially when the tables could be moved aside. The hotel and bar at the West Branch stage stop was one venue for dances and parties, not to mention good food.[105] Lomo, situated along the Humboldt Road, on the ridge overlooking the end of the little railroad, housed a forty- by eighty-foot covered platform for holding dances. A hotel that served meals was also located there. Chico was often well represented at dances in both locations.[106]

One year, there was a lively Fourth of July celebration at Lomo, although it actually took place on Saturday, July 8, since a large portion of the mountain residents traveled to Chico for the holiday. The belated celebration on the ridge was nevertheless a huge success, attracting a very large crowd. One of the festivities included a tug of war between two logging camps, the lighter team from Petersburg against the heavier one from Lomo. After the hard-fought struggle, the boys from Petersburg prevailed. The people honoring our nation's independence that day enjoyed various

Early Logging in Northeastern California

You can bet the thirsty lumber boys took advantage of this establishment at Lomo at least a time or two. The photograph was dated around 1903. *Courtesy of CSU, Chico, Meriam Library, Special Collections. Donated by Alzora Snyder.*

kinds of races too, including one with horses, and other athletic events. The winner of the greased pole–climbing competition was Ike Smith, who was rewarded five dollars for coming out victorious. Naturally, the affair ended with a "grand ball."[107]

They also celebrated Christmas at the mill. One year, a reporter described the festivities that took place in the mill's dining hall. The ladies arranged two fine trees, which were said to be "dazzlingly brilliant" in the candlelight. Evergreens decorated the hall, and there was plenty of music for the partiers to enjoy. L. Hoke, who played Santa Claus, arrived just in time, despite having to make a long trip and contending with bad road conditions to get there. A reporter from the *Chico Daily Record* described the gift-giving time, saying that

> *along with tools, books, candy and dolls for the children, came a host of little creatures, some of them dusky of skin and as short of wardrobes as a ballet girl, and these were labeled for the mill boys. One fine little fellow*

91

in white furs still awaits Jim Smith, and labeled "Klondike." (It is hoped Jim will soon call for it, as the nights are getting pretty cold.)

Much merriment was caused during the distribution of presents, as each recipient was required to "appear in person" in order to receive his "goods," and the advice which went with them from Santa was given gratis.

A fine program was rendered, principally by the little ones, who did unusually well. [108]

Afterward, the people were treated to an oyster and turkey dinner, followed by—what else—a dance. A prize was given to the best waltzer, Mr. Cussick, who won by acclamation, although he did not appear to remember much of it, maybe because he was too engaged in "'shooting the shoots' on a step-ladder." (The phrase "shooting the shoots" referred to the act of riding the log chutes on a homemade craft, much like a flume boat.) It must have been a great time because the celebration didn't end until 6:00 a.m.

A reporter for the *Chico Daily Record* once described a New Year's Eve celebration in which about a hundred partiers celebrated in style at the mill. While engaging in dance, their eyes were treated to "a profuse display of cedar boughs in the shape of an artistically conceived cornice surmounting the upper portion of the rooms, cedar completely usurping the paramount place of importance in the decorations that a once famed lecturer declared belonged to the lily and the sunflower."[109]

To add to the enchantment, a number of large mirrors were positioned about. Just before midnight, the guests all sat down in the dining room to enjoy an elegant meal.

Of course, Thanksgivings were celebrated at the mill also. Although this holiday didn't appear to get as much coverage from the press as Christmas and New Year's, one time it was reported that the mill community gathered together during this celebration for an evening of dancing (no surprise there) to go along with their turkey dinner.[110]

The lumbermen and their families didn't need an official holiday to have a good time. One summer day, they simply held a Sunday picnic on the banks of Little Smokey Creek. The main event for the day was a baseball game between the millworkers and boys from the Little Smokey Creek camp. Needless to say, since the event was held in a rough canyon, the playing field was hardly what one would consider well groomed. In fact, when a player was able to hit the ball hard, it usually resulted in either a home run or a lost ball. The outfielders were positioned so far out that an extra umpire was stationed in the outfield with them, and he had to ride in to report if the player was able to make the catch or not before the base runners were

Early Logging in Northeastern California

This photo shows a log rollway used to load the rail cars from a logging chute near the confluence of Big Chico Creek and Little Smokey Creek. The structure on the right housed the machinery to pull logs along the chute. Believe it or not, somewhere near here they found enough room to play baseball. *Courtesy of CSU, Chico, Meriam Library, Special Collections. Donated by Glenn Dietz.*

allowed to advance. The reporter for the *Chico Daily Record* felt that if it hadn't been for the delays in waiting for the field umpire to return with his observations, the score of the ballgame would have been even larger. As it was, when the spirited game was over, the millworkers had won, 18 to 14.[111] You have to admit, these lumbermen gave "sandlot baseball" an entire different meaning.

Of course, the West Branch Mill families had many other reasons to celebrate too, weddings among them. In 1898, the newspapers reported that two different Shuffleton girls married employees of Sierra Lumber. On May 1, Miss Nellie Shuffleton hooked up with Charles Weber, and on November 22, Miss Etta Shuffleton tied the knot with James Weldon.[112] On February 22, 1902, Dr. Enloe's sister, Martha, married the superintendent of the mill, Frank Thatcher, in Chico. However, the dance hall at West Branch was the scene for a later reception, with 113 friends in attendance. Naturally, a dance was held, and a grand meal was served. Numerous toasts were made, including: "Why Tarry and Not Marry?" by Jay Higgins and "What Is Life Without a Wife?" by Morris Murphy. The party lasted until 7:00 a.m.[113]

Remember Harry O'Neil, the stubborn trial witness who couldn't manage to stay on the flume boat? In anticipation of his approaching nuptials with Miss Robinson, Harry spent months celebrating the upcoming event by building a cozy little cottage at the mill site that he would have ready for her when the time of union arrived. While the pair was in San Francisco getting married, a local newspaper reported that their neighbors planned a big reception back at home. The editor asked his readers to not say anything about it to the newlyweds when they returned through Chico because it was supposed to be a big surprise.[114] Now, if that isn't a switch…The media asking the public to keep something a secret!

What's a story about logging without a good ol' brawl or two? The boys from the woods provided us with a few scrapes that were noteworthy enough to be reported in the news. The first one took place one evening when "Big Bill" Wallace, known as a gambler, showed up at the recently built hotel/saloon at the West Branch stage stop. Bill was a large man who liked to talk with his fists, especially after getting liquored up. Some of the West Branch Mill boys were not there very long before Bill decided to harass a few of them. Although the ensuing encounter didn't even last a minute, the hotel guests found it most entertaining. A reporter for the *Chico Daily Record* described the incident as follows:

> *Finally he directed his abuse to John Lucas, who gave him to understand that he was not to be imposed upon. Wallace said he could change the direction of Lucas' nose, but before he had time to accomplish the feat, Lucas landed a right-hander on his chin and proceeded to place his fists all over the gambler's face. When Lucas had finished with the big fellow he was a fit subject for the army hospital. Wallace is now under the care of a nurse.*[115]

Despite being a fit subject for the army hospital, Big Bill must have been a fast healer because he was ready to tangle with Lucas once more at the same place a few days later. Again, the spectators sided with Lucas, knowing that he was not one to look for trouble but rather was drawn into a fight with the big bully a second time. On the other hand, the crowd knew that Big Bill was a "pug." As expected, Wallace was pummeled again, this time bad enough that Dr. Smith was summoned from Chico to tend to his wounds.[116]

Another fight of interest involved two Sierra Lumber Company employees scrapping it out between themselves one morning while riding the stage back to the West Branch Mill from Chico. Apparently, passengers Ed Ervin and Pat Ryan were feeling pretty good when they left town, but an argument ensued

Early Logging in Northeastern California

This is a photograph of the West Branch Hotel, located along the Humboldt Wagon Road, circa 1900. *Courtesy of CSU, Chico, Meriam Library, Special Collections. Donated by Glenn Dietz.*

Dated around 1903, this photo shows what is believed to be the interior of the West Branch Saloon. *Courtesy of CSU, Chico, Meriam Library, Special Collections. Donated by Alzora Snyder.*

during the long, bumpy ride near the Ten-Mile House. It was not long before stage driver Crain noticed the scuffle and could see that Ervin had a firm grip on Ryan's nose with his teeth. Crain tried to intervene but initially had no luck breaking up the hold with ordinary measures. So he decided the best solution was to twist on Ervin's nose until the angry combatant released his grip on Ryan's nose. Ervin was then told to get off the stage, while Ryan was obliged to ride the stage the rest of the way nursing a very sore proboscis.[117]

Although driver Crain was available to referee the fight on the stage, sometimes the legal system was brought in to ultimately settle the matter. This was the case when Mr. Margraves and Mr. Wright once got into a fisticuff at the mill. The justice court ruled the latter was in the wrong, although it was not clear how the former was ever compensated.[118]

The West Branch Mill once had a visitor, J.F. Nash, who knew how to have a good time on the flume. Nash was a member of a group of four men who were touring the area and photographing mining and timber operations. One member of the group was none other than F.H. Deakin, the man who sold the Sierra Estate that started the Diamond Match era in California. The following photos in this chapter were taken during Nash's little adventure,

Nash leaves the West Branch Mill. *Courtesy of the Bancroft Library University of California, Berkeley.*

Nash passing under the awnings of a couple of buildings placed close together. *Courtesy of the Bancroft Library University of California, Berkeley.*

Nash passing a flume tender station near the valley. *Courtesy of the Bancroft Library University of California, Berkeley.*

with the West Branch lumberyard as his starting point and somewhere in or near the valley serving as an end point.

While we're on the subject of having fun on the flume below the West Branch, there's a story that's been told about one of those support cables that was simply too much of a temptation for a daring visitor from Oakland one day. After a few drinks, the energized adventurer made a ten-dollar bet with a friend that he could go hand over hand down a cable that started at a height of ninety-six feet and stretched out down the canyon about sixty to seventy yards. Apparently, it wasn't long before the daredevil realized that maybe ten dollars wasn't enough for his trouble, but by then it was too difficult to work his way back up. When he finally made it to the bottom of the dangerous descent, his bare hands were quite bloodied and in considerable pain from the rusty cable's many small frayed and broken wires.[119]

Hunting was another favorite pastime for the lumbermen. Undoubtedly, deer, bear and mountain lion were common game, along with smaller animals. However, not all hunting trips turned out to be as enjoyable as planned, such as the time when D.I. Knorr took that nasty fall off the flume (or the Harry Hoyt tragedy, of course). Now, one may think that these lumbermen knew the country well enough to know their way around without getting lost, but that's exactly what happened to Verne Fritter one day while he was out hunting. He started out one morning with a friend named Kellogg, who couldn't keep up with Verne's pace and turned back to head home. When Verne didn't make it back to the mill that evening, the community became quite concerned. They organized a search party, which failed to locate him that night. The following morning, another party was organized, and while they were out looking for him, the exhausted man finally got his bearings straight and managed to find his way back to the mill. Apparently, Verne had become disoriented and wandered about until he realized he would have to spend the night out in the cold, as it was still early in the spring. The lost hunter only had two matches with him, and one of these failed to light. Fortunately, he was able to start a fire with the only one he had left.[120] Verne may not have had a very good time on that hunting trip, but when he made it back to the mill, safe and sound, at least he had plenty of reason to celebrate.

CHAPTER 7

THE END OF AN ERA

A s early as 1904, it was evident that available timber for the West Branch Mill was beginning to run out and the only options for the future were to either extend the railroad or move the mill to a new location. After doing some survey work, it was determined that extending the railroad was cost prohibitive, so plans were set in motion to eventually move operations to a location upstream that was previously logged but still had some valuable timber left to harvest. It was first reported that the new mill would be erected at the site of the old Cascade Mill, near Butte Meadows. At the time, the plans were to abandon the old railroad bed for train traffic and use it as a bed for the lower section of the extended flume instead.[121]

When the West Branch Mill logging season closed in 1905, many workers felt it may have been for the last time. This was the first year that the operations at the mill ceased before the first rains. Nonetheless, the largest cut ever was made that season, almost fourteen million feet.[122] By February 1906, it was a foregone conclusion that it would just be a matter of time before logging in Big Chico Creek would be moved upstream, and now Soda Springs, about ten miles away, was being mentioned specifically as the site for the future operations. Over the winter, a long chute was built upstream from the end of the railroad. In April, boarding and bunkhouses were erected at the new site, and even a saloon opened at the lower end of Butte Meadows, located nearby, for the convenience of the loggers.[123]

Nonetheless, the West Branch Mill was not done producing lumber and had one more successful year left in its tank. Although quality trees were getting harder to reach, the reconstruction of San Francisco and other cities devastated by the recent earthquake in April of that year promoted the need for all grades of lumber, including the lower grades that had been harder to market in the past. The circumstances, which were very unfortunate for others, may have been the difference in whether or not the West Branch was given another year of life. When the mill finally shut down for the last time on October 20, 1906, it had managed to cut up ten million feet of lumber that season.[124]

Unfortunately, the West Branch Mill also had one more significant accident, nine days after it cut its last log. Frank Thatcher was supervising the movement of machinery from the mill when a large timber fell on his leg, breaking two bones just above the ankle. He was transferred to his home, and brother-in-law Dr. Newton T. Enloe was immediately called.[125]

As if to add a final touch on closing out the story of the West Branch logging operations, the land at the site of the mill was eventually transferred to Tehama County in 1944. The arbitrary diagonal line between the two counties that was established prior to that was altered to follow section and property lines instead, which created a situation in which approximately eight square miles of land were exchanged. But take heart, citizens of Butte County: although Tehama County now possesses the location, Butte still owns the history.

While the West Branch Mill was still making lumber in 1906, big plans were well underway for moving the West Branch operations site to Soda Springs as soon as the season ended. (This was Barney Cussick's old stomping grounds—back in 1880, he had a log contract for the Arcade and Belmont Mills.) The new mill was expected to have double the capacity of the West Branch and be equipped with all the modern equipment, including a double band saw. Furthermore, plans were made to develop a town nearby. As soon as the present logging season ended, the transfer of equipment was supposed to begin. Even before it ended, freight teams were hauling supplies from Chico to the new site. By December, it was reported in the news that 150 men were employed in building the new mill and laying down eleven miles of flume. The foundations were already in place, ready for the next step. A smaller mill was in place to supply lumber for construction, getting its logs from chutes that fed into it. The company was optimistic that, although the area had been logged years ago, this plant would be in operation for many years to come.[126]

Before that, however, even bigger plans were in the works. Beginning in 1904, negotiations were underway for Sierra to sell out its entire plant and timber holdings to a group of Minnesota lumbermen, headed by R.W. Turnbull. In 1905, the *Chico Record* was optimistic that the deal would eventually go through, despite the delays. One of the major issues being investigated by the Minnesota group was the feasibility of building a railroad that would go directly from the valley to the timber, thereby eliminating the need for the flumes. By early 1906, however, it was apparent the deal would probably not materialize, despite nearly a year and a half of bargaining. The local papers confirmed it by that spring. Although the price seemed right, it was suggested that one possible holdup was that the investors themselves were differing on how to improve and operate the new venture. Another source indicated that the final estimate of timber was a quarter of a billion board feet less than originally estimated. The intent of Sierra Lumber was clear, however, and the effort to interest other potential suitors was now set in motion. At one time, it was rumored that T.B. Walker, representing the Red River Lumber Company (of Paul Bunyan fame), was interested, but that deal never went through either. Walker already owned a large amount of timber holdings nearby, called the Big Meadows tract, which had been purchased from Sierra Lumber in 1902.[127]

Enter Diamond Match, the next serious group of investors to look into purchasing Sierra Lumber. It made sense because the group owned a large amount of timberland nearby and was already operating the large mills on Magalia Ridge and Chico. Diamond's bid to acquire Sierra's properties was not surprising, considering the company may have already been showing some interest back in 1901, when Fredrick Deakin tried to sell it the Chico division. When the takeover appeared imminent, in early March 1907, the work on the mill at Soda Springs was abruptly halted. Despite the effort already expended, it has been suggested that the building of the mill at Soda Springs was really no more than a bluff made by Sierra Lumber in order to make it look like it wasn't really anxious to sell. Even before the actual move was put into motion, some people speculated that the timber around the new mill would last only a few years. The chapter on Sierra Lumber finally closed officially on March 19, 1907, a few days after the Chico and Red Bluff plants were temporarily closed down, so that Diamond could take inventory of their stock.[128] Soon after the takeover, Diamond shut down the Chico remanufacturing plant, in favor of its Barber plant. However, the buildings at the old Sierra plant were retained and eventually housed a veneer (plywood) plant, the first in California. That didn't last very long, as financial issues and troubles with the gluing process forced the closure of this plant for good in 1909. The Red Bluff factory was permanently shut down in 1911. After the takeover was official, Dr. Enloe didn't waste any time returning to Chico. Within a month, his professional card indicated that he was back in his old Morehead office.[129] He also went on to become the chief surgeon for Diamond Match.

When Diamond Match took over, the flume down Big Chico Creek Canyon was no longer of any use to it, so it was abandoned. When this happened, most of the time these massive structures were left to just rot or be destroyed by forest fires. However, not all of the pieces were wasted. Ranchers apparently used some of the remnants for fence posts to contain their livestock. Furthermore, a few of the more easily accessible portions were dismantled for use in building homes. It's been reported that, in Chico, the Pine Street section of the flume was torn down and used to build an amusement establishment on Flume Street in 1908. The huge dome contained a large swimming tank, a roller-skating rink and a merry-go-round, among other attractions, and was called the Rotunda Bath and Amusement Building. There's a story that George White made a name for himself one day, when he dove from the top of the dome into the water, a drop of eighty feet.[130]

When the West Branch Mill operations finally drew to a close, it was evident that much of the accessible old-growth timber in the northeastern California foothills was beginning to disappear. Recall that the proposed Soda Springs operation was going to resort to working land that had been previously logged

Although this postcard image refers to it as the Rotundo Bath and Amusement Building, most people refer to it as Rotunda. Either way, it's been said that it was constructed from abandoned flume lumber. *Courtesy of Butte County Historical Society.*

Early Logging in Northeastern California

The "Arch" trestle may be long gone, but the landscape in this very rugged and remote part of the canyon remains the same (see page 69). *Photo taken by the author.*

The trestle in the canyon below Ten-Mile House may also be long gone, but the big creek boulder hasn't changed much (see page 70). *Photo taken by the author.*

by the lumbermen. When Diamond Match first started cruising its California holdings, it soon realized that the biggest timber had already been taken.

Of course, this trend had already begun earlier, in other parts of the country, as well. During the latter decades of the nineteenth century, the United States was growing at a very rapid pace, thanks to feverish town building and construction of a seemingly endless network of railroads. Industrial capitalism drove an environment of overproduction in an extremely competitive market, which in turn created a volatile system that promoted an unhealthy timber economy. Overproduction started a vicious cycle, beginning with lowering the price of lumber. To make up for the loss in revenue, the timberland owners would cut more, saturating the market even worse. Another way to offset losses was to cut wages and cut back on labor, never a good thing for the American worker.

To make matters worse, a tremendous amount of unnecessary waste was the byproduct of this behavior. The prospect of immediate profits came first, considerably behind future considerations for a healthy, replenishing natural resource. Early on, much of the virgin timber was just left to rot on the forest floor. When a majestic pine rose to 100 feet or more before the first limb was reached, the common practice was to just take the first few logs and leave the rest behind. (In a 1907 report, Sierra Lumber even admitted that in the early years around Soda Springs, it left more timber on the floor than it took away.) Shake makers had a very bad record, leaving 100,000 feet, in log scale, for every 1,000 shakes that were made from a nice sugar pine. The aggressive work of steam donkeys tore up much of the residual timber, literally turning large sections of land into worthless brush. High-lead logging, practiced in these parts after the West Branch Mill closed down, was extremely destructive also. The devastation left behind often made the land vulnerable to fire and erosion, not to mention disease.

We should not be too quick to condemn the zealous practices of lumbermen during that time period. It was simply part of the culture. While loggers were surely devouring big timber like locusts mowing down a wheat field, they were not the only ones guilty of taking advantage of the previously untapped natural resources of the western states. At this same time, miners were eroding the earth, farmers were depleting the soil and ranchers were overgrazing the rangeland.

By the last quarter of the nineteenth century, the unabated devastation of previously healthy woodlands had already been taking place for several decades, particularly in the eastern states. In fact, it was the dwindling white pine forests of the Great Lake states that eventually drove Minnesota timber magnates—like Chipman, Turnbull and Walker—to search westward for new timberlands to harvest. This increasingly destructive situation spurred some visionaries to start a new movement in the direction of public awareness and action toward the protection of American forests. A man named Franklin B. Hough, who, in 1876, was the first person assigned by the federal government to assess the conditions of the nation's forests, has been credited with essentially setting the wave in motion. In 1881, he became the first chief of the newly formed U.S. Division of Forestry, the forerunner of today's U.S. Forest Service.

Other organizations were also getting into the act. For instance, the American Forestry Association, made up of scientists and private contributors, some of whom were affiliated with industrial wealth, was formed in 1875. Scientific research was beginning to play a major role in ensuring that future forests would be sustainable. By the end of the century, major universities, such as Cornell and Yale, were establishing professional schools of forestry.

In 1891, Congress attached an important rider to a bill designed to revise land laws, which gave the president of the United States authority to establish forest reserves from public domain lands, to be managed by the Department of the Interior. For the next six years, reserves were being set aside, with no plan for management. Finally, in 1897, the Pettigrew Amendment of the Sundry Act defined management for the lands being set aside. With the passage of the act, the purpose of forest reserves became clearer—to provide a constant supply of timber to meet the demands of the American people. Finally, in 1905, Congress passed a bill that transferred the forest reserves from the Department of the Interior to the Department of Agriculture. This was the beginning of the U.S. Forest Service, and the reserves were soon referred to as national forests.

In 1885, California's concern for the health of its timberlands precipitated the creation of the California State Board of Forestry, one of the first to be appointed in the nation. Although it lasted only eight years before it was abolished, its purpose was to collect and circulate important information on forestry, in addition to providing officers to enforce laws. A new State Board of Forestry, with the creation of the state forester position, was approved in 1905.

In the meantime, Chico was doing its part by performing exemplary research in tree growth. In 1888, the Chico Forestry Station was established on twenty-nine acres of land surrounding the area where the Chico Nature Center is located today. It was one of two forest experiment stations created in California around that time, the other being in Santa Monica. John Bidwell, who feared that denuding the slopes of the mountains promoted flooding in the valley, donated the land for an arboretum to the State Board of Forestry. The station was taken over by the University of California (UC) in 1893, when it was reportedly becoming run-down and neglected, aggravating the general considerably. By 1896, however, Inspector Charles W. Shinn, of UC, paid the station a visit and declared that it was once again in good condition. By that time, the station was raising about nine thousand large trees of varying species, including pines. Botanists and foresters from other countries were known to visit the site in order to gather valuable information from its pioneering work. There was even a connection to the Sierra Lumber Company. The flume, which ran along the western edge of the tract, kept the soil under it continually wet to promote the growth of willows and water-loving shrubs. The City of Chico eventually purchased the land, and it is now part of Bidwell Park.[131]

In 1904, the Plant Garden Company was formed in south Chico. One of its contributors was none other than Sierra Lumber Company, along with Annie Bidwell, widow of John Bidwell, and the Diamond Match Company. In 1920, the U.S. Department of Agriculture took over complete ownership

The blister-resistant sugar pine breeding project had to be abandoned by the Genetic Resource and Conservation Center because the species could not handle the harsh conditions of Chico. A small number of specimens remains, but these short and stocky trees don't come anywhere close to resembling the large conifers that can be seen in the nearby foothills. *Photo taken by the author.*

of the 209-acre plant introduction and breeding facility. Many of us who have been around a while remember it as the Chico Tree Improvement Center. Now, however, it's called the Genetic Resource and Conservation Center (GRCC) and is under the direction of the Mendocino National Forest. Among other things, the GRCC creates improved Douglas fir and ponderosa pine seeds for reforestation and restoration. Unfortunately, the sugar pine trees planted for just such a purpose could not withstand the harsh Chico environment.[132]

In addition to donating land for the Plant Garden Company, Annie Bidwell was dedicated to creating a public awareness of the massive forest destruction that was taking place and the need to protect one of the nation's most valuable resources. In 1905, the *Chico Daily Enterprise* reported that she promoted a competition for the best essay written by a Chico Normal student on the subject of forestry. The presentation ceremony for the prizewinners was a gala affair held at the school and attended by about five hundred people. Normal Hall was elaborately decorated with a floral display, and a chorus of at least sixty voices, led by Lida Lennon, entertained the guests. Dr. C.C. Van Liew gave a talk and stressed the importance of educating the young about forest preservation, or as the newspaper put it, "to instill in him or her the desire, the eagerness to see our beautiful and plentiful forests protected from the many enemies who and which try to destroy them in various ways."[133]

Mrs. Bidwell also gave a speech, describing her efforts to mitigate damage done by heavy logging to major forest roads used by teamsters from the mountains to the valley. Chico Normal students submitted three hundred papers. The first prizewinner was awarded a gold medal and the second a silver one. Five others were cited for honorable mention.

The local media was doing its part, too. As early as 1878, the *Chico Enterprise* demonstrated concern over forest destruction, publishing an article warning of impending disaster if unrestricted logging was allowed to continue at the rate it was going. For one thing, the editor was concerned about how removing the trees that protected the snow from the sun's hot rays promoted early and rapid snow melt, resulting in valley flooding. Furthermore, the news noted that mass destruction of forestland would have an effect on local climate.[134] Imagine that. People were even concerned about man-caused climate change back then, over one hundred years ago.

Using the already devastated forests of the eastern and southern parts of the country as an example, the *Chico Daily Record* was praising the work of scientific forestry and the setting aside of large tracts of land as reserves, in hopes of saving the western states from a similar fate. Indeed, the need for the protection of trees was a popular topic in the news media at the turn of the century.[135] Informed people recognized that times had changed, with modern machinery—like evolving donkey engines and logging railways—speeding things up so fast that forest regeneration could not keep up. In 1905, a *Redding Courier* representative was quoted in the *Chico Daily Record* in reference to logging practices in the woods around McCloud, California, north of the Sacramento Valley. The representative couldn't have said it better: "Modern lumbering methods differ vastly from the old days, when Bill Porter and Powers and that old bunch cursed their bulls and made the forests ring with their forcible remarks to the wondering steers that slowly moved the logs to the old slow mills."[136]

Once the damage was done, the forest might never recover. Even if it did, it could require hundreds of years for stands to reach full growth again. Sugar pine, in particular, is susceptible to white pine blister rust, which further reduces the number of very large old-growth trees for that species.

These huge trees in Calaveras Big Trees State Park dodged a bullet. Back in 1945, plans by Pickering Lumber Company to harvest the previously undisturbed grove for sugar pine were prevented by an organized effort of many people. The preserve is now called the South Grove and is one of the few places left where one can still experience a truly undisturbed grove of sugar pines. *Photo taken by Jill Mark.*

Early Logging in Northeastern California

Today, there is a greater awareness of the need for healthy forests, not only to protect against fire, erosion and insect infestations but also to ensure that there will always be enough quality timber for the needs of future generations. Therefore, timber harvesting is now generally conducted in a more responsible way than it was one hundred years ago.

Nonetheless, old-growth forests are not as prevalent as they were at the turn of the twentieth century, and their numbers have been declining ever since. In 1993, an investigation was performed that determined that only 11 percent of the commercial timber cropland (i.e., mixed conifer, true fir and timber pine forest types) in the Sierra Nevada study area was considered old-growth, compared to 45 percent in a 1945 examination. In 1993, mostly all of the old-growth stands were under federal ownership, in either national parks or forests, with less than 2 percent on privately owned land, even though this constituted almost one-third of the coniferous forests in the study area. Yellow pine and mixed conifer stands have been heavily logged

This old-growth, but not undisturbed, pine forest is located just north of where the Pacific Crest Trail crosses Highway 36 in Plumas County. The grove of large trees is managed by Collins Pine of Chester, California, to appear like it did in the pre-settlement period. In 1999, a 580-year-old sugar pine died in this grove, leaving a stump eighty-five inches in diameter. Note the open forest floor. *Photo taken by Jill Mark.*

Remnants of a flume tender's station still exist in Big Chico Creek, below Forest Ranch. It's generally believed to be where the "Palace" once stood. *Photo taken by author.*

in the past, severely impacting their old-growth numbers, but there are still some large trees scattered about. Furthermore, fire control and other factors (e.g., insects) have caused many pine tree stands to be replaced by the more shade-tolerant true firs, which promote a forest floor that is less open and sunny. It's determined that most of the area under private ownership (e.g., where the West Branch operations occurred) will now be managed for non-old-growth usefulness.

Therefore, we may tip our hats to the boys of yore for providing us with such a captivating story about a romantic time in the history of California, when natural resource harvests were bountiful and unrestricted free enterprise was in its heyday. However, we must also accept the sobering fact that the days of vast numbers of those great conifers towering majestically over spacious forest floors may be gone forever. Unless, of course, man and his machines can somehow manage to go on vacation for a few hundred years and leave the landscape with enough time to recover.

APPENDIX

MYSTERIES OF THE FLUME

How Many Flume Stations Were There?

Nellie Weber, one of the three young girls in the sunken flume boat, and noted historian John Nopel, who performed a considerable amount of research on the Big Chico Creek flume, named five flume tender stations—Campbell Creek, Big Feeder, the Palace, China Switch and the Dump. In his research notes, logging historian W.H. Hutchinson listed Sawmill, Big Feeder, Palace, Rocky Point, China Switch and Old Dump. John Nopel suggested the stations were spaced approximately five to six miles apart and located only along the lower two-thirds of the flume. It's possible that these were the most recent stations, maybe those that existed before the final abandonment of the flume in 1907. However, Nellie Weber recalled that the Campbell Creek station was not used after the opening of the West Branch Mill, which makes sense, since Campbell Creek was located just above the junction where the flume spur from the mill met with the main flume. Therefore, the author believes it may have been replaced by the Sawmill station at a spot located lower down on the creek.

It's been suggested that at one time or another, there were many more stations than just these five or six, and findings from an archaeological study conducted by R. Heath Browning, an honors student at California State University, Chico, support this assumption. During his investigation of the stretch between the golf course in upper Bidwell Park and the Big Chico Creek Ecological Reserve (BCCER), located in the canyon below the location of the Fourteen-Mile House stage stop, Browning discovered evidence of seven possible stations along just that eight-mile section of the flume. Furthermore, his findings showed the locations of the stations were not spread out evenly. Two were actually located adjacent to each other. This would indicate that he may have either discovered flume tender cabins that existed at different times during the flume's thirty-two years of operation or that stations were not systematically separated by a particular distance but placed strategically near trouble spots instead. The former explanation may be why there were two places so near to each other in the upper part of the BCCER. Maybe the Palace, which burned down in 1898, was rebuilt, but not at the exact same spot. This might also explain why Nellie Weber remembered it being on stilts, while the site generally accepted today as the Palace has a rock foundation.

The San Francisco news reporter who rode the flume in 1877 recalled passing twelve distinct locations that appear to be stations, almost twenty years before the West Branch Mill began operating: Buckhorn Station, Campbell's Creek Station, the Junction, Big Feeder Station, Buckeye Station, Morris Station, Hot Coffee, Palace Hotel, Road View, Cold Spring, Lazy Man's and Iron Canyon Station. The fact that he did not mention China Switch indicates that it may have been added later or that the naming of it changed over time (more on that later). Since the reporter did not mention seeing a flume tender's station until he was fourteen miles past his starting point, it appears the stations may have been more numerous in the lower two-thirds of the flume, where there may have been more trouble spots.

WERE THE 1877 AND 1886 OFFICIAL BUTTE COUNTY MAPS INCORRECT OR AT LEAST MISLEADING?

The 1877 and 1886 official Butte County maps clearly show the flume crossing Big Chico Creek in section 17 (T24N.R3E.) from the east to west side, when looking upstream. The historical photo of the "Arch" shows the trestle crossing from the west to the east side, looking upstream. Therefore, when this author went in search of the site, he was expecting to find that the old photo was reversed, which sometimes happens when reproducing a historical image. However, that was not the case. The contemporary photo, taken by the author about four and a half miles downstream from the mill, verifies that the trestle actually crossed from the west to the east, looking upstream, contrary to what the Butte County 1877 and 1886 maps indicate.

One plausible explanation is that the route of the flume was changed at some point after the 1886 map was published, and that the Arch photo was taken later. However, the author's personal observation of the location suggests that was unlikely at this particular spot. Another scenario might be that there was

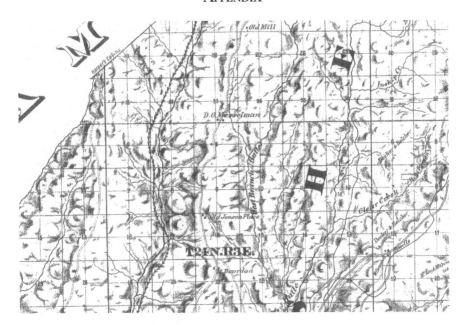

This is a portion of the official map of Butte County, 1877. The map clearly shows that the flume crossed Big Chico Creek in section 17 of T24N.R3E. from the east to west, looking upstream. However, the historical photo of the "Arch" and the contemporary shot of the same location suggest just the opposite. *Courtesy of Butte County Public Works.*

more than one trestle in that immediate area. If so, there had to be a series of no fewer than three to make sense with the crossing shown on the map. Finally, it could be that the maps were simply incorrect. It should be noted that in the September 28, 1877 edition of the *Chico Enterprise* there was some criticism of the 1877 map by some people who claimed that McGann made errors, especially in regard to locations of several properties. However, the description of the flume path was not questioned, to this author's knowledge. Keep in mind, however, James McGann did not survey the Chico Creek flume. Colonel H.B. Shackelford, the surveyor for Tehama County, marked out the line for the construction crews to follow. McGann could only work with the information available to him at the time, which may have been inaccurate.

WHERE DID THE NAME CHINA SWITCH COME FROM?

An article printed in the September 5, 1953 edition of the *Chico Enterprise-Record* may have the answer. Titled "Worried Chinese Cook's Troubles Ended by Flume," the news story was contributed by a man named Tom

Boness. Tom explained how, in the 1880s, a Chinese cook from a mill upstream was once in fear for his life because of some talk he'd overheard. So, the frightened employee made a raft and was on his way down to the safety of Chico, when someone who despised Chinese saw him coming and purposefully threw a switch gate that was designed to dump lumber directly into Big Chico Creek, killing the unfortunate man. (Boness said this was before runarounds were constructed to clear lumber jams.) Hence, the name of the station became "China Switch."

Tom identified the mill upstream as the old Sierra Lumber Company mill, at West Branch. However, that mill was not yet in operation at that time. Despite this contradiction, the explanation may nonetheless have some truth to it, particularly in light of the high anti-Chinese sentiment that existed during those days.

NOTES

The number of sources that the author consulted in researching for this book is too long to list in their entirety. Much of the information can be easily found in the books, history journals and scientific research cited in the bibliography. The author referred to over three hundred old newspaper clippings and a variety of other sources, as well (i.e., W.H. Hutchinson research notes, geology and tree identification books, interpretive trial guides, magazines, maps and county records). For the convenience of those who may want to carry on further research, the author has chosen to list the following notes and references, not found in the bibliography sources, that he feels may be of greatest use to the reader. These include mostly newspaper clippings.

CHAPTER 1

1. Geologically speaking, most of this terrain is considered the foothill and lower mountain region of the most southern portion of the Cascade Range. However, from a forestry perspective, it's often thought of as part of the Sierra Nevada. The mixed conifer belt, which was subject to heavy logging around the turn of the twentieth century, is contained within this area.
2. *Northern Enterprise*, 14 August 1874; *Chico Enterprise*, 31 March 1876.
3. *Weekly Butte Record*, 4 August 1877.
4. *Chico Enterprise*, 23 June 1876.

5. *Chico Enterprise*, 4 August 1876; *Chico Record*, 18 June 1947.
6. *Chico Enterprise*, 8 December 1876.
7. Ibid., 15 December 1876.
8. Ibid., 29 December 1876.
9. Ibid., 9 February 1877.
10. Ibid., 1 November 1878.
11. CSU, Chico, Special Collections, MSS 072, Box 2, Folder 2.
12. *Chico Record*, 17 June 1947.
13. *Chico Enterprise*, 31 August 1877.
14. Sherman Reynolds, "A Ride in a Flume," *The Normal Record* 2, no. 9 (February 1898): 7.
15. *Chico Record*, 11 July 1947.
16. *Weekly Mercury*, 6 July 1877.
17. *Chico Semi-Weekly Enterprise*, 3 December 1880.
18. *Chico Enterprise*, 26 December 1879; *Weekly Butte Record*, 27 December 1879.
19. *Chico Semi-Weekly Enterprise*, 28 May 1880; *Chico Semi-Weekly Enterprise*, 4 June 1880; *Chico Enterprise*, 23 October 1885; *Weekly Butte Record*, 24 October 1885.

CHAPTER 2

20. *Chico Daily Enterprise*, 2 October 1891.
21. *Chico Daily Record*, 25 September 1901, 11 November 1901, 12 September 1902.
22. CSU, Chico, Special Collections, MSS 072, Box 7, #21.
23. *Chico Daily Record*, 30 June 1903.
24. Ibid., 28 August 1897, 9 September 1897, 10 September 1897.
25. Ibid., 18 June 1898.
26. Ibid., 6 December 1897.
27. Ibid., 18 October 1897.
28. Ibid., 5 January 1899.
29. Ibid., 1 July 1898. Although the original franchise had expired and the road was a free public highway by then, Bidwell was still highly involved with its maintenance.
30. *Chico Enterprise*, 8 July 1898.
31. *Chico Semi-Weekly Enterprise*, 10 December 1880.
32. *Chico Enterprise*, 26 July 1895; *Chico Weekly Chronicle-Record*, 27 July 1895.
33. *Chico Enterprise*, 15 March 1895, 1 November 1895; *Chico Weekly Chronicle-Record*, 2 November 1895; *Chico Enterprise*, 28 February 1896; *Chico Daily Record*, 2 January 1903, 10 November 1904; *Chico Record*, 16 January 1917.
34. *Chico Daily Record*, 22 November 1905.

35. *Chico Record*, 28 June 1947.
36. *Chico Daily Record*, 5 November 1900, 17 December 1900; *Chico Enterprise*, 21 December 1900.
37. *Chico Enterprise*, 20 November 1896.
38. Ibid., 25 October 1901; *Chico Daily Record*, 24 June 1902.
39. *Chico Daily Enterprise*, 18 April 1910.

Chapter 3

40. *Chico Daily Record*, 20 May 1899; *Chico Enterprise*, 26 May 1899; *Chico Daily Record*, 29 August 1899, 9 November 1899.
41. CSU, Chico, Special Collections, MSS 072, Box 2, Folder 1.
42. *Chico Daily Record*, 24 June 1902, 23 March 1904, 10 May 1904, 19 August 1904.
43. *Chico Chronicle-Record*, 1 November 1896; *Chico Semi-Weekly Record*, 31 July 1900.
44. *Chico Weekly Chronicle-Record*, 20 June 1896.
45. *Chico Enterprise*, 17 July 1896.
46. *Chico Daily Record*, 22 May 1902, 23 May 1902, 26 May 1902.
47. *Chico Semi-Weekly Record*, 31 July 1900; *Chico Enterprise*, 31 August 1900.
48. *Chico Daily Enterprise*, 17 December 1904; *Chico Daily Record*, 4 October 1905.
49. *Chico Daily Record*, 16 February 1904, 6 April 1904.
50. Ibid., 28 April 1904, 19 August 1904.
51. Ibid., 11 October 1904, 14 October 1904.
52. *Chico Daily Enterprise*, 23 January 1906; *Chico Record*, 23 January 1906.
53. *Chico Daily Record*, 15 September 1904.
54. Ibid., 20 August 1905.
55. Ibid., 12 December 1898.
56. Ibid., 14 November 1903.
57. Ibid., 20 May 1904.
58. Ibid., 9 April 1900.
59. Ibid., 13 May 1905; *Chico Daily Enterprise*, 13 May 1905.
60. *Chico Daily Record*, 1 December 1904, 2 December 1904.
61. *Chico Enterprise*, 26 July 1895.
62. *Chico Daily Record*, 14 November 1905.
63. Ibid., 6 July 1897; *Chico Enterprise*, 26 August 1898.
64. *Chico Enterprise*, 9 August 1901; *Chico Daily Record*, 13 August 1901, 5 December 1901; *Chico Enterprise*, 5 December 1901.
65. *Chico Enterprise*, 25 September 1903.

NOTES TO PAGES 59–76

CHAPTER 4

66. *Chico Daily Record*, 9 March 1899.
67. Ibid., 13 June 1901, 14 June 1901; *Chico Enterprise*, 14 June 1901; *Chico Daily Record*, 18 June 1901; *Chico Enterprise*, 21 June 1901.
68. *Chico Daily Record*, 20 June 1905; *Chico Daily Enterprise*, 20 June 1905.
69. *Chico Record*, 18 October 1906.
70. *Chico Daily Record*, 17 May 1905; *Chico Daily Enterprise*, 17 May 1905.
71. *Chico Daily Record*, 23 November 1901; *Chico Enterprise*, 29 November 1901. Before starting for the mill, Kingston called ahead on the telephone to ask where the train was located and was told that it was "taking on a load of wood." He thought this meant a load of wood for the mill, so he assumed the train was going downhill. However, the man at the other end meant wood for fueling the locomotive before it started the uphill climb. A simple miscommunication...that's how accidents happen!
72. *Chico Daily Record*, 28 August 1903.
73. Ibid., 18 July 1901; *Chico Enterprise*, 19 July 1901.
74. *Chico Daily Record*, 17 October 1904; *Chico Daily Enterprise*, 17 October 1904.
75. *Chico Weekly Chronicle-Record*, 14 December 1895.
76. Ibid., 15 June 1895.
77. *Chico Daily Record*, 23 November 1897.
78. Ibid., 1 September 1905.
79. Ibid., 11 May 1903.
80. *Chico Record*, 8 August 1906; *Chico Daily Enterprise and Chico Post*, 8 August 1906.
81. *Chico Record*, 9 August 1906, 10 August 1906; *Chico Daily Enterprise and Chico Post*, 10 August 1906.
82. *Chico Record*, 11 August 1906; *Chico Daily Enterprise and Chico Post*, 11 August 1906.
83. *Chico Daily Enterprise and Chico Post*, 11 August 1906; *Chico Record*, 12 August 1906, 14 August 1906, 21 August 1906; *Chico Daily Enterprise and Chico Post*, 21 August 1906.

CHAPTER 5

84. *Chico Daily Record*, 24 February 1902; *Chico Enterprise*, 28 February 1902; *Chico Enterprise-Record*, 22 December 1954. There appears to be a difference of opinion, in regards to which sister, Emma or Martha, initially came to California with the doctor.

85. *Chico Daily Enterprise*, 25 September 1905.

86. *Chico Daily Record*, 19 May 1903.

87. *Chico Enterprise*, 14 June 1901; *Chico Daily Record*, 24 June 1901, 9 July 1901, 22 August 1901; *Chico Enterprise*, 14 March 1902.

88. *Chico Daily Enterprise*, 18 October 1905; *Chico Daily Record*, 19 October 1905.

89. *Chico Daily Record*, 18 June 1901; *Chico Enterprise*, 21 June 1901.

90. *Chico Daily Record*, 19 June 1901.

91. Ibid.; *Chico Enterprise*, 21 June 1901.

92. *Chico Daily Record*, 20 June 1901.

93. Ibid., 21 June 1901.

94. Ibid., 27 June 1901.

95. Ibid., 23 July 1901.

96. Ibid., 26 July 1901.

97. Ibid., 1 August 1901.

98. Ibid., 10 October 1901.

99. *Oroville Mercury*, 8 October 1901, 9 October 1901; *Chico Daily Record*, 9 October 1901; *Daily Register*, 9 October 1901; *Chico Daily Record*, 10 October 1901; *Daily Register*, 10 October 1901; *Chico Enterprise*, 11 October 1901.

100. *Chico Daily Record*, 12 October 1901; *Minutes and Orders* 7, Superior Court Butte County, 1901–1905, 68–69.

101. *Chico Enterprise*, 18 October 1901; *Minutes and Orders* 7, Superior Court Butte County, 1901–1905, 76.

102. *Chico Daily Record*, 31 December 1901; *Chico Enterprise*, 3 January 1902; *Minutes and Orders* 7, Superior Court Butte County, 1901–1905, 96.

103. CSU, Chico, Special Collections, MS 072, Box 7, #19.

104. "Badgered Doctors," *Time* 16, no. 8 (25 August 1930): 51.

CHAPTER 6

105. *Chico Daily Record*, 18 June 1898; *Chico Enterprise*, 17 May 1901; *Chico Daily Record*, 18 May 1904.

106. *Chico Daily Record*, 23 August 1900; *Chico Enterprise*, 4 July 1902; *Chico Daily Record*, 9 September 1902, 13 August 1904.

107. *Chico Daily Record*, 11 July 1905.

108. Ibid., 28 December 1897.

109. Ibid., 2 January 1900.

110. *Chico Enterprise*, 5 December 1902.

111. *Chico Daily Record*, 22 August 1905.

112. Ibid., 2 May 1898, 24 November 1898. The May 2 paper spelled the last name of the groom "Webber." However, the Butte County Recorders Office *Index to Marriages Men 1893–1920* indicates that the last name was actually spelled "Weber."

113. Ibid., 24 February 1902; *Chico Enterprise*, 28 February 1902; *Chico Daily Record*, 5 March 1902.

114. *Chico Daily Record*, 23 March 1905; *Chico Daily Enterprise*, 25 March 1905.

115. *Chico Daily Record*, 11 October 1898.

116. Ibid., 17 October 1898.

117. Ibid., 22 September 1905.

118. *Chico Daily Enterprise*, 31 October 1905.

119. *Chico Record*, 17 June 1947.

120. *Chico Daily Record*, 2 April 1905.

CHAPTER 7

121. *Chico Daily Record*, 3 August 1904.

122. Ibid., 11 November 1905.

123. *Chico Record*, 2 February 1906, 21 April 1906.

124. Ibid., 3 May 1906, 24 October 1906.

125. *Chico Daily Enterprise*, 30 October 1906; *Chico Record*, 30 October 1906.

126. *Chico Semi-Weekly Enterprise*, 10 December 1880; *Chico Record*, 26 September 1906, 14 October 1906, 24 October 1906, 21 December 1906.

127. *Chico Daily Record*, 14 January 1905, 25 February 1905, 12 March 1905, 25 June 1905; *Chico Record*, 24 February 1906; *Chico Daily Enterprise and Chico Post*, 2 May 1906.

128. *Chico Record*, 8 March 1907, 20 March 1907, 21 March 1907.

129. Ibid., 10 April 1907.

130. Ibid., 31 July 1947.

131. *Chico Enterprise*, 30 November 1894, 19 June 1896; *Chico Chronicle-Record*, 20 September 1896.

132. Interview, handouts and email from Robyn Scibilio, site manager Genetic Resource and Conservation Center, Chico.

133. *Chico Daily Enterprise*, 9 December 1905.

134. *Chico Enterprise*, 6 December 1878; *Chico Daily Record*, 10 September 1897, 3 December 1902.

135. *Chico Enterprise*, 24 April 1903; *Chico Daily Record*, 23 December 1904, 12 March 1905.

136. *Chico Daily Record*, 22 July 1905.

BIBLIOGRAPHY

Beardsley, Debby, Charles Bolsinger and Ralph Warbington. *Old-Growth Forests in the Sierra Nevada: By Type in 1945 and 1993 and Ownership in 1993.* Washington, D.C.: United States Department of Agriculture, 1999.

Borden, Stanley T. "Sierra Lumber Company Beginnings of the Diamond Match Company in Northern California." *Western Railroader*, no. 345 (November 1968).

Bowles, Laura. "Dr. Newton Thomas Enloe." *Tales of the Paradise Ridge* 9, no. 1 (June 1968).

Browning, R. Heath. "The Big Chico Creek Flume: An Archeological Reconnaissance." Undergraduate honors project for CSU, Chico College of Behavioral Social Science, 2003.

Chang, Anita L. "A Historical Geography of the Humboldt Wagon Road." Master's thesis presented to the faculty of California State University, Chico, Spring 1991.

Clarke, K.W., ed. "The Humboldt Road." *California Folklore Chico Collection*, *vol. 14.* N.p.: Chico State College, 1958.

Coy, Owen C. *California County Boundaries: A Study of the Division of the State into Counties and the Subsequent Changes in Their Boundaries.* Revised edition. Berkeley: California Historical Survey Commission, 1973.

Guinn, James Miller. *History of the State of California and Biographical Record of the Sacramento Valley, California. An Historical Story of the State's Marvelous Growth from Its Earliest Settlement to the Present Time.* Chicago: Chapman Publishing Co., 1906.

Hodges, Gerald L. "The Development of the Enloe Hospitals: 1902 to 1937." Paper written for history class at California State University, Chico, 1958.

Hutchinson, W.H. *California Heritage: A History of Northern California Lumbering.* Revised edition. Santa Cruz, CA: Forest History Society, Inc., 1974.

————. *The California Investment: A History of the Diamond Match Company in California.* N.p., 1957.

Kratville, William W., ed. *The Car and Locomotive Cyclopedia of American Practices.* Sixth edition. Omaha: Simmons-Boardman Books, Inc., 1997.

Labbe, John T., and Vernon Goe. *Railroads in the Woods.* Berkeley, CA: Howell-North, 1961.

MacKay, Donald. *The Lumberjacks.* Toronto: McGraw-Hill Reyerson Limited, 1978.

Mansfield, George C. *History of Butte County California with Biographical Sketches of the Leading Men and Women of the County Who Have Been Identified with Its Growth and Development from the Early Days to the Present.* Los Angeles: Historic Record Company, 1918.

Nopel, John H. "The Sierra Lumber Company Flume in Chico Creek Canyon." *Butte County Historical Society Diggin's* 12, no. 4 (Winter 1968).

Robbins, William G. *Lumberjacks and Legislatures Political Economy of the U.S. Lumber Industry, 1890–1941.* College Station: Texas A&M University Press, 1982.

Robertson, Donald B. *Encyclopedia of Western Railroad History.* Caldwell, ID: Caxton Printers, 1998.

Shover, Michele. "Chico's Lemm Ranch Murders and the Anti-Chinese Campaign of 1877." (1998). In *Exploring Chico's Past...And Other Essays.* N.p.: Xlibris Corporation, 2005.

Stephens, Kent. *Matches, Flumes and Rails: The Diamond Match Company in the High Sierra.* Corona del Mar, CA: Trans-Anglo Books, 1977.

Taylor, Will L. *The Sierra Flume and Lumber Company of Northern California: With Descriptive Material Prepared by W.H. Hutchinson.* N.p., 1956.

Weeks, David, A.E. Weislander, H.R. Josephson and C.L. Hill. *Land Utilization in the Northern Sierra Nevada.* Berkeley: University of California, 1943.

White, John H., Jr. *American Locomotives: An Engineering History, 1830–1880.* Revised edition. Baltimore, MD: Johns Hopkins University Press, 1997.

Williams, Richard L. *The Loggers.* Alexandria, VA: Time-Life Books, 1976.

INDEX

ABOUT THE AUTHOR

Andy Mark worked as a brakeman and conductor on the railroad for twenty-one years before going back to college. He graduated from California State University, Chico, as a double major in mathematics (option in statistics) and psychology and now works as a statistical consultant and data analyst. He is acknowledged in books and scientific publications  for his contributions. He is a member of the Butte County Historical Society and wrote an article titled "1859 Butte Creek White Settler–Indian Conflicts" that appeared in the society's spring 2010 edition of the *Diggin's*.

An avid hiker and student of nature since he was a youth growing up in northern California, Andy first started showing interest in the history of the lands he was walking through after becoming captivated by the story of Ishi, the last documented "wild" Indian in North America. As he explored the backcountry of Butte and Tehama Counties, Andy began looking for traces that people and events left on the land, which began an adventure of research that led to the writing of this book.

Visit us at
www.historypress.net

Printed in the USA
CPSIA information can be obtained
at www.ICGtesting.com
LVHW022150141023
761116LV00005B/110